THE LIVELY PLACE

THE
LIVELY PLACE

Mount Auburn,
America's First Garden Cemetery,
and Its Revolutionary and
Literary Residents

STEPHEN KENDRICK

Illustrations by Matthew A. Longo

Beacon Press, Boston

Beacon Press
Boston, Massachusetts
www.beacon.org

Beacon Press books
are published under the auspices of
the Unitarian Universalist Association of Congregations.

19 18 17 16   8 7 6 5 4 3 2 1

This book is printed on acid-free paper that meets the uncoated paper
ANSI/NISO specifications for permanence as revised in 1992.

Text design by Yvonne Tsang at Wilsted & Taylor Publishing Services

Library of Congress Cataloging-in-Publication Data

Kendrick, Stephen
The lively place : Mount Auburn, America's first garden cemetery,
and its revolutionary and literary residents / Stephen Kendrick.
pages cm
Includes bibliographical references.
ISBN 978-0-8070-6629-4 (pbk. : alk. paper)—ISBN 978-0-8070-6630-0
(ebook) 1. Mount Auburn Cemetery (Cambridge, Mass.) 2. Cemeteries—
Landscape architecture—Massachusetts—Cambridge. 3. Cemeteries—
Landscape architecture—Massachusetts—Watertown. 4. Cambridge (Mass.)
—Buildings, structures, etc. 5. Massachusetts—Biography—Anecdotes.
I. Unitarian Universalist Association. II. Title. III. Title: Mount Auburn,
America's first garden cemetery, and its revolutionary and literary residents.
F73.61.M8K45 2016
929'.5—dc23   2015031468

Dedicated to

CAROLINE LOUGHLIN

Whose love and knowledge of
Mount Auburn's landscape and design
made this book possible

CONTENTS

It is an easy case to make that Mount Auburn, founded in 1831, is one of the most beautiful places in America, and that its long history as the world's first rural cemetery and America's first rural garden cemetery is important, and that many of the nation's most venerated writers, artists, scientists, reformers, troublemakers, and gadflies are buried here in impressive numbers. But in wandering through its circuitous roads and hidden-away garden cul-de-sacs, you can easily and quickly lose the sense of just how small Mount Auburn really is. Among revered world cemeteries, it is a jewel.

It is a small thing, originally only 72 acres, now 175, with some 98,000 graves. One of the inspirations for Mount Auburn is the great Pere-Lachaise Cemetery in Paris, with over a million graves, where you can visit the resting place of Wilde, Balzac, Chopin, Proust, and even Jim Morrison of the Doors.

Other notable cemeteries include Woodlawn in the Bronx, site of more than 320,000 graves on 400 acres, and Duke Ellington besides.

Arlington National Cemetery, the home of the Tomb of the Unknown Soldier and where the Eternal Flame flickers over the slain Kennedy brothers, has 400,000 graves on 624 acres.

The stars burn the brightest at Forest Lawn outside of Hollywood with Sam Cooke and Sammy Davis Jr., as well as Elizabeth Taylor and her friend Michael Jackson; it has 240,000 tombs over 317 acres.

These American cemeteries, as impressive as they are, are minuscule compared with Manila North in the Philippines, which has more than a million graves, and Wadi al-Salaam in Iraq, five million graves. As resting places, they are massive. What is Mount Auburn compared to them?

As I worked on this book, Mount Auburn was burnishing its credentials on many fronts. If I merely listed its recent awards, grants, and designations, in a sense the book would write itself. Most impressive is the 2003 designation of the cemetery as an official National Historic Landmark, a rare status granted to only 2,500 places in the entire country. The

status does not come easily; nominated properties must meet stringent criteria for having "exceptional value or quality in illustrating" our heritage.

The honor makes official something that those who understand our cultural history have long known: this small spot of land has had a remarkable influence across our history, as recognized by the official wording on the metal plaque now posted on the inner wall of Jacob Bigelow's great Egyptian Gateway: "Established in 1831 as the nation's first large scale designed landscape open to the public, Mount Auburn was the first American rural cemetery. It initiated the great age of American cemetery building and influenced the design of public places, monuments, and suburbs."

As impressive an accomplishment as this is, it still does not explain the entirety of Mount Auburn's allure.

Mount Auburn has recently been designated a Level III arboretum, due to its strong horticultural staff and large collections of plant specimens. Beautiful and environmentally sophisticated new greenhouses have been built, a crucial step toward the goal of eventual recognition as a Leadership in Energy and Environmental Design site from the US Green Building Council.

Also giving a sense that Mount Auburn is in a period of renewal is a recent collections stewardship grant from the Institute of Museum and Library Services, recognizing the importance (and fragility) of thirty of its most significant monuments, and enabling staff to document and digitize primary materials from the vast historical collections. In effect, Mount Auburn is now seen as an important historical museum, nurturing a notable art collection besides.

Designation of the rolling and lush landscape as an Important Bird Area by the Massachusetts Audubon Society, and the increasing tide of more than a quarter of a million visitors each year—birders and so many more walkers—add to a feeling of revitalization everywhere.

All this, and it remains an active graveyard.

These functions combine to reinforce one another, adding resonance and a certain romance to the ground. I have come to think of the different aspects of Mount Auburn as facets of a diamond, each surface catching light and reflecting it back enhanced. This small jewel of a garden has helped shape our history and promises to do so in a new era. These 175 acres are not only hallowed ground but are increasingly relevant to a nation in ecological crisis.

When I was a student at Harvard Divinity School more than thirty years ago, my wife, Liz, and I took frequent walks along these paths, like generations of young people before us have. I little dreamt that one day I would ever write about the people—famous, infamous, and obscure—who surrounded us. It impressed me as a wonderful place to escape the pressures of urban Cambridge, but I knew very little about it. On my way to seminary, I had encountered only a brief mention of it in cultural historian Philippe Aries's *The Hour of Our Death*, probably the most influential book of the last century on the subject of death. Aries pointed to the 1831 creation of Mount Auburn as a crucial turning point in how mortality was viewed in our modern age, and as a harbinger of death's beautification, where "the tomb is eclipsed in the landscape." In fact, Mount Auburn signaled a change whereby a cemetery could be viewed as a "romantic oasis." On first encountering its lovely rolling vales and dells I saw no reason to argue the point. It was true; death never looked so good. Visiting became a relaxing, peaceful respite, but truthfully, after moving away from Cambridge, I ceased to think much about my lovely place of escape.

Some years later, I was a bit shocked reading Gary Wills's

Lincoln at Gettysburg and encountering the author's lofty evaluation of Mount Auburn's place in American life. Wills helped me recall times there with heightened appreciation. As the jacket copy states, "In the space of a mere 272 words, Lincoln brought to bear the rhetoric of the Greek Revival, the categories of Transcendentalism, and the imagery of the 'rural cemetery' movement." In recalling Edward Everett's speech preceding Lincoln's, Wills brings to life that era's devotion to Greek rhetoric, and he describes how the battlefield cemetery they were dedicating that day recalled not only Athens's Kerameikos graveyard, but also Mount Auburn. As Wills put it, Everett was "not only a celebrant of American battlefields; he was also a connoisseur of American cemeteries. He had participated in the creation of Mount Auburn, the Cambridge cemetery that became one of the principal cultural institutions of the nineteenth century." William Saunders, a Scottish horticulturalist, was deeply influenced by Mount Auburn in his design for the Gettysburg National Cemetery and in his work on the setting for Lincoln's tomb in Springfield's Oak Ridge Cemetery three years later.

In iconic settings that drew power not only from the sacrifices of fallen warriors, but also from the beauty of nature, Everett and Saunders both explicitly evoked Mount Auburn's New England philosophical underpinnings: "The contemplation of nature that rural cemeteries were meant to foster was a threshold experience for the Transcendentalists. The horizon, where heaven touches earth, suggested the interplay of the ideal with the real." That generation's belief in the absolute intermixture of Soul and Nature and indwelling Divinity, an American dream called Transcendentalism, found in Mount Auburn's creation an expression of that thin horizon.

Here at Mount Auburn, one comes as close as possible to the energy of early America, held under the sway both of

Transcendental visions and of the promise of a nation as a new Eden. The philosopher John Locke wrote, "In the beginning, all things were America." Founder John Winthrop said, in his "City on a Hill" sermon to those huddled on the ship *Arbella*, that they went to found "a watered garden." Those who created Mount Auburn were doing more than burying their dead or creating the nation's first rural cemetery—they were self-consciously establishing a living symbol of what they believed America to be.

In the vibrancy and energy of the new republic, anything was possible. The artist Thomas Cole summed up the way antebellum Americans saw their new land: "We are still in EDEN; the wall that shuts us out of the garden is our ignorance and folly." In a toast for the new venture, the founders of Mount Auburn raised their glasses to "Eden—the first abode of the living—Mount Auburn, the last resting place of the dead. If the Tree of Life sprung from the soil of the one, Immortality shall rise from the dust of the other." General Henry A. S. Dearborn, who oversaw much of the original design for the cemetery's grounds, described the first seventy-two acres of "Sweet Auburn" landscape as nothing less than a new Eden.

In antebellum America, it seemed that everyone eventually came to see the calming splendors of Mount Auburn, from young students at nearby Harvard (Emerson wrote of wandering the new cemetery to "let what would pass through into the soul"), to famous foreign visitors, such as the nineteen-year-old Prince of Wales, who ceremonially planted two trees. Perhaps the most insightful was the intrepid English social theorist Harriet Martineau, who ended her book on young America by expressing sheer delight in Mount Auburn, seeing it as a repudiation of pious New Englanders, "whose fathers seemed to think that they lived only in order to die." No, this innovative vista was something more. She proclaimed, "Mount Auburn is the most beautiful cemetery in the world."

For a place so renowned for its antiquity and historical resonance, Boston has in fact been astonishingly profligate with its history, leaving few historic sites standing, few vistas unaltered. In her book *Lost Boston*, Jane Holtz Kay wrote in 1980 of these losses and how they accumulate "never with so much reckless abandon as in our own generation. So much of historical Boston is gone." But four miles west of the city lies one of our remaining opportunities to reenter that past, at a garden not so much lost in time as having been formed lovingly by it.

Moving through the imposing gray gateway today, one enters a designed landscape representing, in a real way, the hopes and visions of our ancestors, citizens of a proud young republic. Each generation since the founding of Mount Auburn in 1831 has left its mark on this historic landscape, yet its quiet roads and winding, forested paths eventually take you, once you have learned the ways of this verdant labyrinth, toward the hidden heart where it all began, Consecration Dell. In the opening service to mark Mount Auburn's creation, Joseph Story, then an associate justice of the United States Supreme Court, spoke for all: "What is the grave, to us, but a thin barrier dividing time from eternity, and earth from heaven?" That day, September 24, 1831, over two thousand citizens surrounded him in the silent green-shrouded dell, believing that something new was being created here.

After one has been touched by the beauty of the landscape as a whole, one slowly begins to narrow down, to see each grave as adding grace and melancholy beauty to the whole. Each one bears a story—every lot a family saga, every carved statue a testimony, each engraved stone a life.

The Lively Place presents a new way to envision the people who dwelled, for a time (even as the nation stumbled into the cataclysm of the Civil War), in the allure of "the Newness," the sense that it could do and create anything, that this American prospect was no phantasm but an instrument by which to transform the world. Mount Auburn was, and remains, the place where that dream was made real and given form, where we can visit and see their vision today.

I came to think that maybe I wasn't writing a book about a cemetery at all, but rather about an array of dynamic souls caught up in a generation that believed it lived on the cusp of history—the era of Transcendentalism, innovation, invention, and reform. While researching, I stumbled on Talbot Hamlin's recent assessment of the era's architecture. Note the tone—almost Emersonian: "It was as if man in America, around 1820, had rediscovered his five senses, had suddenly, like one breaking through from the forest to sun-drenched, sea-bordered towns, all at once become conscious of bright sun and distance and freedom."

Imagine what that antebellum generation must have felt, intoxicated by the allure of America, this new Eden. Mount Auburn was not a place of death so much as a distilled essence of where divinity and human energy met and then dwelt. The citizens of Boston believed they were shattering a wall of ignorance, particularly as they embarked on transforming brute realities of death and burial. The energies of this new time were directed everywhere in a tidal wave of reform and revelation fit for, in Emerson's words, "this American, this new man." The era of stacked piles of moldering bones, hastily interred in the crowded churchyards of Puritan times, was over. As life was being transformed, so too was death.

There is something else as well, though not as readily apparent as its beauty, that makes Mount Auburn an important American place. We have had a long struggle to come to terms with the founding ideal that "all men are created equal," and this has been nowhere as true as in our places of burial. We have segregated ourselves by race, religion, and class when we come to place our dead into the ground—as if unaware that it is, in the end, mortality that truly binds us as one.

Mount Auburn is a significant place if only because its founders in 1831 dared to create a space where no one was to be excluded, or sectioned off in death. Free blacks, Jews, the rare renegade Roman Catholic—people of all faiths, economic classes, and circumstances were welcomed. William Clendaniel, president of Mount Auburn from 1988 to 2008, often said that Longfellow the poet is buried here, true—but so is Dexter Pratt, the blacksmith he wrote about. To which I add that the previously enslaved Mary Walker, who bought and lived in that same blacksmith's home on Brattle Street, was in turn buried here as well. Death is the ultimate democracy, and Mount Auburn's creators had the genius to make this idea real.

The Puritans maintained that God had given us two scriptures: one, the Bible, and two, the scripture of Nature itself, a Created space that spoke volumes. Mount Auburn, in its fusion of mortality and the endless sweep of seasons, forcefully reminds us that this old sensibility has never been completely lost. We Americans still possess an abiding sense that, as art historian Angela Miller noted, we see our nation as "a great book of Nature." This is a little book about the greatest narrative of all.

Blanche M. G. Linden's vast, exhaustively researched *Silent City on a Hill* will remain Mount Auburn's history of record, and I noted with sadness and appreciation the announcement of her death as I completed this book. Anyone who approaches this topic can only build a little knoll upon her great mountain. So this book is meant to be short enough to allow you to read it quickly and lively enough to hold your interest—and even to be cheerful besides—since a book about a cemetery needs that higher perspective to make its way into the world. A long, serious history has already been written, and survives for those who wish to delve deeply.

But if you love Mount Auburn, or are perplexed by its hold on you, or just want, in a swift perusal, an overview of why this place is less haunted than hallowed, more inspiring than depressing, and why it is, in the end, one of the most beautiful places in America in all seasons, then my hope is that you'll find much to ponder in these pages. You can get a great deal out of Mount Auburn simply by walking its paths, going along with one of the dedicated guides, listening to a guided tape in your car, poring over informative maps and colorful pamphlets, and noting chalk notations in the alcove of the Egyptian Gateway about what birds have appeared this week. But in a short compass, this book tells you a bit about how the place came to be, how it continues to be cultivated, and why it is an ecological garden of growing importance. It also introduces you to some of the most interesting people buried here (who are not necessarily the most famous). This is not a guidebook, nor a linear history, but—like this landscape itself—a winding and circling collection of paths that encompass natural history, cultural history, biography, interviews, and personal ruminations. Themes appear only to be obscured by new vistas, then circle back again, like the garden labyrinth of Mount Auburn itself.

I was far along in my research when it became clear that writing a book about a cemetery that happened to be a garden, a designed landscape, an arboretum, a museum, a wildlife preserve, a bird sanctuary, and a repository of the bones of many of America's most important progressive thinkers and reformers would be the ultimate in microhistory. This little graveyard, located on the border of Cambridge and Watertown, Massachusetts, is the brainchild of a small circle of reform-minded Boston philanthropists and is actually a pivot point for seeing America's attitudes toward death, yes, but more importantly, for seeing how we choose to live our lives in nature and in community. It is a place where our attitudes to ecological change could be traced, assessed, and understood.

As the historian Aaron Sachs asks, If you want to write a history of our attitudes toward nature, why stop at Yosemite? Referencing Ken Burns's television series *National Parks: America's Greatest Idea*, Sachs wrote in a *Boston Globe* op-ed that little Mount Auburn was our country's "Second Greatest Idea." Our standing in nature, Sachs believes, depends more on the survival of urban garden landscapes than on our vast tracts of wilderness, as spellbinding as they are. It turns out that Mount Auburn has as much to say about our ecological future as it does about our cultural past.

Of course, in making such claims and surveying this history, it must be admitted that humility was never one of Boston's strengths. There is the old story of a Boston man being given Shakespeare's plays to read for the first time; the giver is trying to convince the Bostonian that the bard of Stratford was a genius. The Brahmin came back, admitting that Shakespeare was indeed an excellent writer. How good? "Why, as I read them, I realized not more than twenty men in Boston could have written those plays!"

That a place as compact as Mount Auburn can cram in

so much of life and liveliness and still remain an oasis is amazing; that it does so in the midst of ninety-eight thousand graves makes it a place of paradox and depth. Gertrude Stein once said of Oakland, California, that "there is no there there." Mount Auburn, it turns out, contains about as much thereness as a place can pack within small limits.

More than a century and a half after Mount Auburn's founding, the Reverend Peter Gomes summed up the founders' "splendid enterprise": "A cemetery ought to be a place where the living and the dead mix on happy and useful terms. This is described as a place of repose and so it is, but it is also a place of purpose, and that purpose celebrates life and beauty, nature and the mysteries of God, which the theologians themselves cannot even begin to express or understand."

This is a landscape both time-bound and timeless, where history and the eternal each speak their truth. Of course, other cemeteries hold their remarkable dead, known or forgotten. Other gardens are as beautiful. Other arboreta have a greater array of specimens. Mount Auburn's distinction is the way these things flow together, the way they are held in balance. Yes, it is a place of peace, of repose. But the title *The Lively Place* was not chosen in gentle irony—this is a garden designed by its founders to awaken fellow citizens to a higher Divinity dwelling within Nature. They wished, as well, to heighten a sense of our mortality within Nature's unrelenting urgency, and our proper place within that power.

The survival of this clear intent is why, I believe, so many people flock here today, and why Mount Auburn still speaks to us not only of life's beauty and briefness, but of the surging energies of a young nation. Yes, this is a landscape of contemplation. But what takes hold in us here is the restless and relentless pulse of history. Fused with the constantly changing sights of sky, blowing trees and grass, swooping birds, and glinting water—all of which give this vista its strange power—there is much here to quicken the deadest and most benumbed spirit. In the end, I don't know a place quite as enlivening as Mount Auburn. It always serves to give me back a sense of life.

This book, I hope, will also give you some sense of how much dedication and determination it takes to hold this fragile ecology of disparate elements together. It amazes me every time I enter Mount Auburn that it is all still here, seemingly eternal but in fact far from it. As the old marble statuary melts in the region's acid rains and snow, as funeral and grieving customs change, as the migrating patterns of birds shift, and as increasingly rare amphibians silently slide into the vernal waters to breed one more year, it all feels, once you have come to love the place, a daunting project to keep all of this—each small piece of it—flowing into another year.

AUTUMN

Autumn: New England's residing glory, what people from all over the world come to see. Maybe we are used to it, or simply through familiarity do not realize our trees produce the greatest profusion of fall color in the world—but there it is.

Nowhere else in the world are concentrated such orange-tinged russets, golds, and vivid reds. Our trees do us proud. There is only a short time to see all this; "leaf-peepers" are simply seekers of something rare and ephemeral. Mount Auburn, although a small player within these thousands of miles of burning fall tints, asserts itself every year as one of the special sites in the midst of nature's color show.

Knowing the science behind it all does not steal away the intensity. Why do New England trees shine so brightly now? Dr. David Barnett, president of Mount Auburn and a horticulture specialist, may have many responsibilities as he runs the cemetery, but he remains an inveterate lover of all things botanical. He does not seem to mind my ignorance, since it allows him to reflect upon what he enjoys.

"The reason the colors are so intense here in New England? It's all a natural process. The shorter day triggers the reduction of chlorophyll, which produces the green, and when this happens, the yellow pigments that have been there all along are revealed. The reds are a different matter, they are called"—and he patiently spells it out for me, aware by now that he is not dealing with a nature man—"anthocyanin pigments, which are produced by a variety of environmental conditions and are at their best in the years when there are bright sunny days and cold nights in the fall. We also have to be fortunate in terms of moisture (something New England usually gets in abundance). If it is a time of drought, the colors dim; frankly, the leaves fall before they have a chance to turn. We just happen to be in the right temperate zone, the right elevation, the right palette of the right kind of trees, particularly our maples."

But with the end of fall comes the fall of all this splendor. While everyone else is gobsmacked by the blinding beauty of autumn, Dennis Collins, horticultural curator, and Paul Walker, superintendent of grounds, are seeing something else; they are scrambling against the reality of winter to finish every project that they have started. Walker supervises an augmented grounds crew to deal with the coming deluge of leaves from over five thousand trees.

In the old days, they would vacuum leaves, three thousand yards full, but all this has changed in the new Mount Auburn. It is still a lot of work, but the whole process is now shrewdly ecological. By late October they stop mowing the lawns and begin mulching the leaves as they start to fall. Having learned over the years the sound ecological reasons for leaving behind grass cuttings, they have concluded it makes more sense to mulch the leaves in place. The mowers are outfitted with mulching blades to pulverize leaves, again and again. The grounds are then ready for winter, and mulched for spring.

The grounds crew uses these cooling months to find the plants they will soon need, and then gets ready to do a great deal of planting in the spring. It is a time to think through good designs for gardens and flowerbeds, and every aspect of a spring half a year away. And they are on the lookout for the first snow that will stick, generally in late December, with the long freezing spells that signal winter is upon them. Like the flitting monarch butterflies around Willow Pond and the Washington Tower wildflower meadow, now at its peak, birds are migrating south. The fall pilgrimage is not like the intense colorful splendor of spring's journey, but slower, stretched out, the colorful mating plumage now molted and muted. Though more birds, accompanied by their young, are making the trip, the effect is now calmer, and birders flock to the grounds in a relaxed, almost reflective way. They search the skies for sparrows, chickadees, juncos, and even rare finches, and as the last of the migrating birds depart, some fifty species remain, readying themselves for the cold to come.

Chrysanthemums bloom late, offering a last burst of color to the chilling landscape. The first sign of spring at Mount Auburn is generally the yellow bud of the witch hazel. Showing the steady, sturdy dutifulness of nature, the last blooming shrub of autumn is the witch hazel again, its last effusion a fragile yellow bloom, a farewell after the limbs of the sugar maples and their kin are shorn.

Consecration Day

There have been several great red books that changed history—there was Chairman Mao's little red book that transformed, and traumatized, China in the last century; Carl Jung's famed red book that was hidden away until reprinted to acclaim in 2009; and, let us not forget, Frodo's Red Book of Westmarch (perhaps better known to you as *The Lord of the Rings*). It turns out I had a little red book, one that would change my life, though I did not properly appreciate it at the time I received it.

More than a decade ago, after I spoke at a Mount Auburn event, my gratuity was a small red book. I popped it into my coat pocket. Rediscovering it weeks later, I noted it was packed with bylaws, regulations, reports, and old speeches from the early years of the Mount Auburn enterprise. I quickly consigned it to the chaos of my office library.

I found it years later as I began to envision this book, and so I settled down to belatedly read my gift. Written and edited by Jacob Bigelow, the book was originally published in 1859. As it turned out, my previous perusal of *A History of the Cemetery of Mount Auburn* had been far too hasty. I immediately slipped into another world. What had seemed pedantic years before changed: the founders' effort suddenly came to life vividly, in precise detail.

Many of the following chapters find their genesis in that

little red book, with its tales from another time. And it all starts in a place called Consecration Dell. One of the most interesting tales in the book is, for me, an account of the improbable gathering that defined the beginning of Mount Auburn in our cultural life. When the Massachusetts Horticultural Society purchased George Brimmer's seventy-two acres of woodland, called "Sweet Auburn" by local students and neighbors who loved to wander through its dense green shade on summer days, no one could have guessed the immediate impact that sale would have.

Even today, after nearly two hundred years of illustrious history, I find it difficult to believe that more than two thousand people joined together in the consecration ceremony. On September 24, 1831, they somehow found their way four miles west of Boston, across the Charles River, to the edge of Cambridge verging into Watertown. Once there, they made their way deep into the very center of the densely wooded area. The vast crowd of New Englanders gathered for a reverent service, which, though nonsectarian, would be intensely imbued with near-mystical fervor. The huge crowd was silent as people settled onto makeshift wooden benches arranged in an oval around the natural amphitheater of the small dell. Their pent-up idealism must have been palpable.

Reading the words spoken and sung that day, we sense the vast gap between their vision of death and ours. The men most responsible for the day—George Brimmer, Dr. Jacob Bigelow, and General Henry A.S. Dearborn—were clearly tapping into latent needs, and the citizens of Boston responded almost instantaneously. Death, with its ability to take a child at a moment's notice (it is estimated that a third of deaths before 1850 were children), felt so close to them. If the rhetoric and intensely romantic response to death seems alien to us, it is because we have the protections of modern medicine, and a chosen emotional distance from mortality's most brutal effects, to insulate us.

In going back to Consecration Day, we can begin to understand what was important, indeed, transcendent to them, and what this forest glen represented: a foretaste of eternity.

The fact that the cemetery's first president, Joseph Story— a renowned judge widely known for his incisive legal mind but also for a poetic sensibility that thrilled all who heard him—had been chosen to make the address no doubt heightened the anticipation. Story was a former congressman, a Harvard Law School professor, and a famed jurist, and he was equally famous for his conversation, which was incessant, witty, and heartfelt. His son said of him, "His real exercise was in talking."

There had been freshening showers the night before, and the morning dawned clear and bright. The *Boston Courier* account, oft quoted in Mount Auburn histories, called the day "one of the most delightful we ever experience at this season of the year." The reporter was clearly moved by what he saw that day, from the "perfect silence of the multitude," which made Story's address ring out clearly, to "the effect produced by the music of the thousand voices which joined in the hymn, as it swelled in chastened melody from the bottom of the glen, and, like the spirit of devotion, found an echo in every heart, and pervaded the whole scene." By the close of the ceremony, the writer concluded, "Mount Auburn has been but little known to the citizens of Boston; but now it has become holy ground."

A great deal changed in the course of that service in the dell. Story's address has a grand style that is foreign to us, yet it still speaks with force and with an appealing humanity. Historian Louis Masur writes movingly of Story's difficulty in facing the challenge of speaking at the event. Just five months earlier, his ten-year-old daughter had died of scarlet fever. " 'Sunk in utter desolation and despair,' Story had admitted that 'life would be to me a burden, a grievous burden, if it were not for the belief in another and better state of existence.' Still, thoughts of her returned him to a state of 'settled and miserable gloom.' "

Thanks to its pervasive sincerity and directness, Story's address remains the true founding document, a suitable preamble to a long history to come. The intent is stated plainly: "It is the duty of the living thus to provide for the dead." No matter what poetry he quotes, or which sentiments on which he takes wing, Story attempts always to speak to the heart, to our common lot. He evokes "the broken fragments of memory" as he traces the history of this duty to the dead, from the "barrows, and cairns, and mounds of ancient times," to the Egyptian, Hebrew, and Greek modes of mourning and caring for the dead.

The latter he spends some time on, because the tradition of Greek city-states interring outside city walls is an important precedent for what Mount Auburn was doing: "They discouraged interments within the limits of their cities; and consigned their relics to shady groves, in the neighborhood of murmuring streams and mossy fountains, close by the favorite resorts of those who were engaged in the study of philosophy and nature, and called them . . . CEMETERIES, or 'Places of Repose.' "

The appeal of the sylvan woods of Sweet Auburn was firmly tied to the idea that, in beauty, loved ones would rest in blessed sleep. This would have been the first use of the word *cemetery* in America; before Mount Auburn, burial places were simply called graveyards.

Story then shifts his focus from history and meditation upon the dead to what this new form of memorial can mean to the living: "They may preach lessons, to which none may refuse to listen, and which all, that live, must hear." It is not out of pride or vainglory that "we should erect columns, and obelisks, and monuments, to the dead," but so that we could sense "our own destiny and duty." We deepen our own senses of our paths when we visit and listen to the lessons those before us wish to bestow. The beauty of the site offers peace and solace as we learn.

This all may be a new idea, a novel way of doing things, but Story wanted to be clear what they were all witnessing that day—"A rural cemetery seems to combine in itself all the advantages, which can be proposed to gratify human feelings, or tranquilize human fears; to secure the best religious influences, and to cherish all those associations which cast a cheerful light over the darkness of the grave."

This was a man who had lost five children, who would soon be interred in the lot he had already bought. His words that day were not mere rhetoric, but a spoken challenge against powers of despair and loss that we can only guess at. And he was supremely eloquent when he described what casts this "cheerful light"—he lists "the forest-crowned height; the abrupt acclivity; the sheltered valley; the deep glen; the grassy glade; and the silent grove. Here are the lofty oak, the beech . . . the rustling pine, and the drooping willow;—the tree, that sheds its pale leaves with every autumn, a fit emblem of our own transitory bloom."

All of these surround them, and will in seasons to come, "as if we were in the bosom of a wilderness, broken only by the breeze . . . or by the notes of the warbler pouring forth his matin or his evening song." For me, the whole oration is bound up near the close with a short, stark sentence very unlike the winding, cursive ones that precede it: "Here let us erect the memorials of our love, and our gratitude, and our glory."

Joseph Story will always remain an important part of Mount Auburn's story as a founder present at the cemetery's creation and as its first president, serving for ten years. He remains the youngest man ever appointed to the Supreme Court, at age thirty-two, and would have been chief justice but for President Andrew Jackson, who called him "the most dangerous man in America." To Jacksonians, Story was entirely too fond of supporting the structures of federal government and the rights of property. As a Unitarian, Story stoutly defended individual rights, particularly religious freedom. His literary flair made his legal writings the backbone of American jurisprudence and made him a hugely popular orator who evoked strong emotion.

Young English visitor Harriet Martineau offered another view of Story's love of this place at the end of her three-volume *Retrospect of Western Travel*, in a final chapter set at Mount Auburn. (Later, she would write the straightforward assertion: "I believe it is allowed that Mount Auburn is the most beautiful cemetery in the world.") It would be Justice Story who gave Martineau a long, personal tour of the cemetery. Martineau was a keen observer with an evident fondness for America and a probing sociological acuity—in fact, she is often credited with being the first sociologist.

When she saw Mount Auburn, it seemed to sum up for her something important about America's truest impulses. "A visitor from a strange planet, ignorant of mortality, would take this place to be the sanctum of creation. Every step teems with the promise of life. Beauty is about to 'spring up out of ashes, and life out of the dust': and Humanity seems to be waiting, with acclamations ready on its lips, for the new birth." For Martineau, visiting only seven years from its creation, Mount Auburn represented a radical departure from traditional mourning rituals. In the course of the warm August afternoon visit, Story took her to the site where five of his children were laid. He showed her where he had delivered the opening address—the small, already hallowed dell. She later recalled that the speech must have been a "beautiful composition, full of the feelings natural to one who was about to deposit here a rich heart's treasure, and who remembered that here he and all who heard him were probably to lie down to their rest."

In 1896, architect Willard Sears designed a red stone administrative building, adorned with a large new chapel in English Perpendicular style, a structure later named for Justice Story. It is where grieving families come to this day to buy a new lot, or to check on the "perpetual care" (in the traditional cemetery phrase) of old plots. It is also where researchers and historians come to access the large cemetery archives overseen by the current curator of historical collections, Meg L. Winslow. Few visitors go past the high desk separating the office area from the public inquiry space, much less into the president's calm corner office, with its windows overlooking Fountain Avenue.

David Barnett, a man I have never seen without a smile on his face, sweeps me in and offers me copies of the Master Plan, one of the most impressive accomplishments of his predecessor, Bill Clendaniel. He praises the vision of Clendaniel, who oversaw a multiyear effort to bring Mount Auburn into the modern age by assessing what needed to change and what needed to be retained, renovated, and renewed. But the Master Plan effort was about more than assessing how the past was to be preserved; it involved figuring out creative ways for a historic landscape to have another hundred years of vitality.

Barnett generously shares his vision of ecological sustainability and his pride in his staff's accomplishments in moving toward that difficult goal, as well as his fervent love of the landscape under his care. And he regales me with a fascinating story about the reclamation and reconstitution of the most precious piece of ground in Mount Auburn. Consecration Dell is, as writer Christopher Leahy put it, more than a secluded hollow; it is a residual sign of the retreat of massive ice sheets eleven thousand years ago, a classic example of a "kettle hole depression in which the ice had been deep enough to leave a perfect little pool at the bottom."

The dell is nearly the exact center of the cemetery on a map, and it is the heart of the place. Being a dell, it happens to contain a vernal pool, which, as Barnett explains to me, is a water feature not fed by other sources—it fills as winter melts into spring, and can often dry up by autumn. Vernal pools are disappearing all over New England. They are fragile and ephemeral things. Not only could this pool die, but by extension, Consecration Dell could lose its central beauty.

When Barnett arrived to help Clendaniel implement the recommendations of the Master Plan in 1993, the whole area was in desperate need of renewal. They decided that, in essence, they would take on a decades-long project to enhance the entire historic area. If they could, they wanted to reproduce what the dell was like on that sunny September morning when Story articulated the dream of Mount Auburn.

Barnett adds, "We decided to restore it, and we knew it would be a long effort. First of all, we had to take out invasive trees that were choking the light and spreading everywhere. Not only that, these Norway maples had not been there, and were not native woodland trees. So we needed to take many of them out (and some of our birders were nervous about that), and replace them with new trees that reflected that time and place. Once the Norway maples were removed, we had to replant native species of ground cover and shrubbery, and by doing that, allow the wildlife inhabitants to return, make the place alive and attractive. We also thought that this would eventually make Consecration Dell an even better bird habitat. We wanted to bring history and ecology together."

Recalling the woodland restoration, Barnett brings up the subject of salamanders. He remembers talking to Clendaniel, at the start of the plan's implementation, about the salamander population, and how it was severely threatened. Yes, the entire Consecration Dell area had to be reclaimed and somehow conserved, but the potential loss of spotted salamanders seemed to represent the dire nature of what they were facing. Vernal pools are extraordinarily rare things, and if the salamanders were threatened, then so was the dell itself. This was the period when the country was beginning to realize that not only were its wetlands precious, but they were severely imperiled—and this tiny pool was the most fragile kind of wetland of all. The dell was historically significant and the emotional heart of the place, and something needed to be done.

Barnett was glad the old stone curbing surrounding the pond had been taken out decades ago, but the entire area was still a problem. There were few native ferns, no suitable ground covers, and, worse, invasive tall trees such as Norway spruces and Japanese barberries had taken over the hillsides, choking out light. These plants were problematic in and of themselves, but what really made them disagreeable was that they simply hadn't been there in 1831. Horticulture curator Dennis Collins, Barnett, and former director of horticulture Claude Benoit (now retired) vowed, wherever it made both horticultural and cultural sense, to return as much as they could to native woodland grounds—from trees, to shrubs, to the pool itself and all its living inhabitants.

Believe me, I never dreamed that spotted salamanders would be part of this book. I started with dreams of writing about figures like Margaret Fuller and Buckminster Fuller (which I do, later), but these seven-inch-long amphibians have squirmed their way into my focus in a big way. The staff are delighted to inform me that the salamanders are no longer endangered and that, once a year on a rainy spring night, the male and female salamanders somehow know that the time for mating has come. Normally, these black and yellow spotted amphibians have been covertly slithering away in hidden underbrush and sodden leaves all over the garden, enjoying meals of worms and insects, when that inner signal arrives. They head down the slopes to the one place that matters, the vernal pool. (Apparently, a small but dedicated group of amphibian watchers, not yet outnumbering the thousands of birders, await a text message from one of their dedicated crew that the salamanders are on the march, then they head into the night rain to assess the situation, flashlights in hand.) There, the salamanders mate, observed or not.

The males retreat from Consecration Dell first, leaving the females to stay behind to lay the fertilized baseball-sized egg sacs, which they attach to sticks floating in the water. One recent count showed 750 egg masses suspended in the pond, a remarkable figure. In two months, the eggs hatch, if they have not been eaten as a delicious snack by herons. And still, the little ones have a tough struggle ahead as they grow and, with luck, leave the pool to head up the hillside for a mature salamander's existence. As long as the pool is preserved, they will continue to return.

Barnett's staff has also spearheaded an effort to reintroduce wood frogs and toads to the ecology of the dell. (There are no fish; vernal pools do not have a ready reliable source of inflowing water, so they mostly dry up in the late summer months.) There is a hope that the reintroduction of the tiny American toad will take hold. Hundreds of toads have been placed all over the cemetery. So far the signs are good that they will breed and, like the salamanders, establish themselves in the ecosystem and glory of the dell. A suspicion that toads had been absent from the grounds for many decades was the sad baseline assumption, but lately the spring call of male toads has happily been heard at both the dell and at Halcyon Lake. If toads are indeed reaching breeding age, the hope is that they are successfully spreading all through the grounds. A toadlet is actually smaller than your fingernail, but this is a big development in the reclamation of the dell.

Turtles, raccoons, foxes, and other creatures also come to enjoy the waters. As the whole Consecration Dell area is re-planted and made more vital, more and more species of birds, especially dozens of varieties of warblers, return and make it their migratory home. There are always red-tailed hawks and great horned owls hovering about, ready to snatch the odd chipmunk if they can get it. With the new shrubbery and ground cover taking hold, wood thrushes and ground-nesting birds are also hovering about. It turns out doing good things for salamanders is good for everybody.

By 2003, the funding and the willpower came together. More than four hundred native trees and shrubs have been added to the mix, and nearly four thousand wildflowers and ferns, along with native ground cover, have been painstakingly planted and nurtured at the four-acre site. The work on this "reconstruction" of an old landscape is not finished, but each year more progress is made. Several hundred trees and shrubs have been planted, and thousands of smaller plants, including native ferns, asters, phlox, and other shade-loving woodland flowers.

But just replanting was not enough—the staff had to get on top of the increasingly difficult erosion problems. The south side of the dell is so steep that the water runoff can sweep away plants and erode precious soil, which is harmful to the vernal pool. So massive work was needed to redo old walking paths (also called "switchback" trails) that traverse the high slopes. The team came up with an ingenious solution: instead of using lines of timber to halt further erosion, they used rolled burlap tubes filled with compost. Inserted plants take root, and the tubes absorb water and hold on more efficiently along the path's edge.

Now the pool is healthier than it has ever been, and though the project is far from completed, it is clearly a success. The slow effort is working. Barnett proudly describes the return of the great horned owl. Virtually everyone I interviewed turned at some point to this effort, and although I am far from a naturalist, I immediately saw why this was so. It is one thing to halt the destruction of an endangered landscape—it is even more exciting, and exacting, to be able to recreate a landscape that was presumed to be gone forever.

Barnett tells me of a public presentation marking the 180th anniversary of Story's address, and how Barnett was asked to speak after powerful excerpts from the address were read by a local guide and actor. He felt moved hearing his words joined with the judge's, forming a unified picture of what all of the staff were trying to achieve. "To say that it was a 'privilege' does not adequately describe how inspired I felt to be standing on the exact spot that Justice Story stood," he recalls.

Barnett admits that when he came to Mount Auburn in 1993 as director of horticulture after a long career in arboretum and public garden management, he only really noticed the trees and flora under his care. The monument and cemetery aspects mostly passed him by. Then, two years on, he was talking in the dell to an old friend, a professor, about a particular Japanese *Stewartia* tree, and as he noted its memorial plaque, a woman walking by came over to him. She introduced herself as the daughter of the woman named on that very plaque.

"She enthusiastically told me that Consecration Dell was one of her mother's favorite spots, and thus she and her siblings had chosen to purchase this tree plaque to remember her in this location. The woman said she came here frequently to think about her mother and it was always an uplifting experience," recalls Barnett. "I have never forgotten that moment, and from that day forward I have understood the importance of the 'cemetery services' that we provide to families as much as I have realized the significance of our horticultural and preservation activities."

And then he shares with me a more personal memory, recalling when his brother asked Barnett to perform his wedding ceremony. Barnett was happy to do so as a one-day-permit justice of the peace. To his surprise, the couple wanted the service on the grounds of the cemetery. This is not as odd as it seems, as there are generally at least twelve wedding services a year at Mount Auburn. The bride wanted the service in the dell and the groom at the top of Washington Tower—so Barnett split the difference, beginning the service deep by the pond, reading Story's words and raising a toast to remember family members who had gone before. Then the wedding party climbed to the high tower, and Barnett married them by the tower's wildflower meadow, overlooking all of Cambridge and Boston.

"It was a wonderful day!" Barnett beamed.

In Story's address, the justice asked his listeners in the deepest dell to gaze high above them, up on the steep hillside, where would be built the great high observatory tower they would dedicate to George Washington: "Ascend but a few steps, and what a change of scenery to surprise, and delight us. We seem, as it were in an instant, to pass from the confines of death, to the bright and balmy regions of life."

From Crypt to Garden

For centuries, burial was a brutal and dispiriting reality, a grim and begrimed prospect for nearly all, even when burial took place in the shadow of a church. Churchyards grew increasingly crowded as the population rose while ecclesiastical precincts could not expand.

Nathaniel Hawthorne, during his years as a diplomat based in Liverpool, England, wrote of finding a crumbling old gravestone by a church near Leamington Spa: "It seemed as if the inmate of that grave had desired to creep under the church-wall. On closer inspection, we found an almost illegible epitaph on the stone, and with difficulty made out this forlorn verse: 'Poorly lived / And poorly died / Poorly buried / And no one cried.' "

The American novelist observed that this grave was on the shady and damp side of the church, endwise toward it, with its headstone within about three feet of the foundation wall so that, unless the deceased man was a dwarf, he must have been doubled up to fit into his final resting place. No wonder his epitaph murmured against so poor a burial as this! "The gravestone is so overgrown with grass and weeds, so covered with unsightly lichens, and so crumbly with time and foul weather, that it is questionable whether anybody will ever be at the trouble of deciphering it again."

It was increasingly the lot of souls to face a fate of being so "poorly buried."

Today, as we walk about the closely groomed and romantic green yards of churches and cathedrals, it is difficult to wrench our minds back to a quite different reality, when bodies literally worked up through the soil and bones protruded from the church ground, even as more holes were being dug to take in the next deluge of the local dead.

We all have heroes, and one of mine is the writer Bill Bryson. He seems to be able to take any topic and render it in remarkably funny prose that delights and edifies in equal measure. While he isn't buried at Mount Auburn (nor, thankfully, anywhere yet), when I stroll Mount Auburn I think of him because he made it abidingly clear, in a way I had never realized, just how nightmarish burial must have been. Racing through *At Home*, Bryson's book on the history of our domestic lives, I wasn't looking out for such stern stuff when I came to the chapter on gardens. At first he described plants and sunshine—all lovely. Then he commenced explaining why, in nineteenth-century England, churchgoers often could not make it through an entire service: they needed to go outside and attempt a breath of fresh air because of the overwhelming stench of rotted corpses in the church burial ground, or from the crypt below.

For example, London in the early 1800s had only 218 acres of burial grounds, and most of that was packed closely around local parish churches. "St. Marylebone Parish Church packed an estimated one hundred thousand bodies into a burial ground of just over an acre. Where the National Gallery now stands on Trafalgar Square was the modest burial ground of St. Martin-in-the-Fields church. It held seventy thousand bodies in an area about the size of a modern bowling green, and uncounted thousands more were interred in the crypts inside." What this meant was that virtually every shovel dig exposed bone, and worshippers often were overcome with noxious fumes. There just was not enough space or dirt to go around, so mourners often refused to attend a burial: "The experience was simply too upsetting, and widely held to be dangerous in addition."

T. S. Eliot wrote, "I will show you fear in a handful of dust." People of the nineteenth century had more than a handful of dust to fear, as New England was no exception to these nightmarish burial traditions. English burial customs were naturally transferred to Boston, and little had changed in the new world.

Mount Auburn's beauty and solace is inescapable. In writing about it, it is easy to occasionally slip into an elevated and romantic reverie that escapes the brute truth of the place—that it is a repository of moldering bones and dry ash, no matter how artfully conceived and tended. Proper appreciation of the emotional impact of Mount Auburn requires an ability to hold these two ideas in balance.

But we are all fairly well practiced in this, especially in regard to death. I have, as a minister, had occasion to ruefully quote an anecdote I found in the *Oxford Book of Death*, in which a spiritualist asks a bereaved mother where she thinks her daughter is in death. She answers, "Oh, well, I suppose she is enjoying eternal bliss, but I wish you wouldn't talk about such unpleasant subjects."

After centuries of accepting this shocking state of affairs, in the mid-1820s, a few visionary Bostonians quietly began to converse among themselves, wondering if something might be done concerning this most unpleasant of subjects—for sanitation and health, and out of decent respect for the dead. The honor of conceiving the possibility of a place such as Mount Auburn goes to William Tudor, a 1796 graduate of Harvard University and founding editor of the *North American Review* who, in 1820, proposed that the city of Boston purchase rural land outside of Boston for a garden burial ground. Mayor of Boston Josiah Quincy was interested in burial reform and formed an advisory committee in 1823 to look into such matters—but no action was taken by the Boston City Council at the time. There matters stood for some years.

Dr. Jacob Bigelow, a member of the mayor's burial committee, decided to convene a small group of friends at his home on Summer Street in 1825 to discuss the state of graves and tombs and decent respect for the dead in Boston. He wanted to alert them to "gross abuses" that needed some creative solution, and he thought he had a splendid idea, born of his love of country walking. "Cherished by the character of my earlier pursuits," Bigelow wrote later, his love of nature "had long led me to desire the institution of a suburban cemetery, in which the beauties of nature should, as far as possible, relieve from their repulsive features the tenements of the deceased."

The response was so positive that the group set out to find a tract of land. Bigelow stuck to the plan even when a first attempt to buy land in Brookline fell through. More fruitless years went by, and opposition to burial reform in the city actually increased, if anything. In this period, the Massachusetts Horticultural Society formed with General Dearborn as its first president. Dearborn invited Bigelow, whom he had gotten to know on the Bunker Hill Monument Committee, to be the society's secretary. Like Bigelow, Dearborn had a penchant for dreaming large—he wanted to create an experimental garden that would bring credit to the society and the new nation's farming techniques. Bigelow saw an opening, so he brought before the horticultural society the innovative (though as we shall see, fragile) notion of joining of these two idealistic ideas at the same future plot of land. In 1830, the society agreed to sponsor just such a venture.

It was then that Bigelow was contacted by a fellow horticultural society member, a man who will forever remain the godfather of the enterprise due to his astonishing generosity, George Brimmer. The local businessman had recently acquired a large tract known as Stone's Woods, the famed "Sweet Auburn" woodlands so beloved of Harvard students. He had bought more farmland along the public road to expand, and protect, the beautiful land between Cambridge and Watertown. Brimmer wondered, would this land fit Bigelow's vision? Brimmer was determined to find a way, one way or another, to preserve the expanse of woods. He was willing to sell the woods to the committee at his original price, though he could have made a killing selling to other local speculators. The new society, bare of funds, immediately started selling subscription lots for burial in the proposed cemetery.

Institutional progress was fine, but the battle for Boston's hearts and minds still needed to be won and stubborn old cultural practices somehow shifted. From Bigelow's little red book comes a heroic address designed to accomplish just this, delivered by the man universally considered the greatest orator of his time, Edward Everett. (Though some later thought Frederick Douglass outshone him.) In Bigelow's history, the author generously gives fulsome credit to Everett, a man who often does not receive acknowledgment; in fact, he is often derided and ridiculed by historians for not properly living up to his resume. On paper, Everett seems a figure impossible to even imagine: minister, congressman, senator, governor of Massachusetts, ambassador to Great Britain, secretary of state, professor of ancient Greek and later president of Harvard, Constitutional Union Party candidate for vice president (he and John Bell lost to Lincoln), preserver of George Washington's Mount Vernon—and yet he is seen in most biographies as a near failure.

Worse, he had the historical bad luck of speaking for two hours before Lincoln's Gettysburg Address, a handy club for historians to beat him with across the decades. (Actually, it remains a good speech, written under a hard deadline; thoroughly researched, completely memorized, and delivered under severe health duress. Everett died fifteen months later. It wasn't his fault that Lincoln then delivered a masterpiece. Everett immediately wrote Lincoln a letter of charming praise, saying, "I should be glad if I could flatter myself that I came as near to the central idea of the occasion, in two hours, as you did in two minutes.")

Everett's style shines deftly in his message to the people of Boston in 1830, as he sought to convince them the old ways of stuffing churchyards with bodies had to change, and that a new mode of burial was at hand. He made the rolling hills of "Sweet Auburn" sound enticing, alluring—a place where you would want your loved ones to reside. But he reserved his elocutionary firepower for the increasingly distressing conditions of burial inside the city itself. In a resigned tone, he admitted what all knew, that "too little thought has been had for the decent aspect of our places of sepulture. . . . Our burial places are, in the cities, crowded till they are full; nor, in general, does any other object . . . than that of confining the remains of the departed to the smallest portion of the earth that can hide them."

Though Everett was the point man for this effort, and although he would be years later buried in the cemetery he helped make possible, he was not, in fact, to be the man who quietly and persistently, over many decades, nurtured this new idea into realization. When other early supporters dropped away, Bigelow stood as the prevailing force, as he was at a meeting on November 23, 1830, at the Exchange Coffee House in Boston. There, a committee was charged with selling the lots and planning Dearborn's experimental garden that would share the space of "Sweet Auburn." By June 1831, they had nearly enough sales money in hand to formally buy Brimmer's land for $6,000, under the auspices of the horticultural society.

It had been seven long years. Bigelow later noted the public's "lukewarm" reaction as the daring enterprise had begun, but what counted in the end was that there were more than enough prominent, and quite wealthy, idealists signing up their families to be buried in this untrammeled lot of forest. When the Commemoration Service at the Dell was held fifteen months later, Mount Auburn was, against all odds and long discouragement, a sudden success.

In writing *Sarah's Long Walk*, a saga about the desegregation of Boston schools from the 1840s all the way to the historic *Brown v. Board of Education* decision, my son Paul and I had to handle a complex historical narrative spreading over 140 years, from the recorded beginnings of the Roberts family all the way to the Supreme Court and Thurgood Marshall.

We needed to make vivid literally dozens of figures. An odd thing happened as we went: we had to shift our focus from Sarah Roberts's family when we discovered a virtually forgotten figure. It is a distinctive pleasure to attempt to right a historical oversight, and highlighting Robert Morris—the first black lawyer to win a jury case and the second to pass the bar—not only gave our book its frame, but its hero. I wondered, the more I learned about him, why there was no statue to him anywhere in Boston.

And now, the same thing had happened again as I worked on this book.

There are so many distinctive and fascinating people buried at Mount Auburn, with its 180 years of history and ninety-eight thousand "residents," and yet there is no doubt who the main figure is, who presides over all. It seems strange that this man is almost completely forgotten today—the good Dr. Jacob Bigelow.

The bare facts of Bigelow's involvement only dimly convey his importance, from his initiative in convening the first organizational meeting, to his tenacity in holding on to the idea of burial reform in Boston, and his role in influencing the design of the cemetery (along with General Dearborn—more on him and their split anon), along with his authorship in 1859 of an account of its early history and his leadership as president of Mount Auburn from 1845 until the Civil War. He designed the Egyptian Gateway that greets (or intimidates) you as you enter, the imposing Washington Tower, and the great granite Gothic Bigelow Chapel. For his closing act, he designed and oversaw the carving of the Sphinx, which for me signifies the mystery and the allure of life's final questions. You can easily locate Jacob Bigelow's death monument, but the reality is that his influence is everywhere at Mount Auburn, just as English architect Christopher Wren's son inscribed in St. Paul's Cathedral: "Reader—if you seek his Monument—look around you."

Like Robert Morris, Bigelow has no Boston statue, though there is a little-remarked-upon bust of him, looking fairly glum, at Mount Auburn today. There is no biography of him. I have come to suspect the reason no one has picked up this task is that, to do the job properly, an author would have to be as knowledgeable about Bigelow as Bigelow was in so many fields of endeavor. Bigelow represents the last generation that could reasonably claim to have authoritative knowledge in virtually every field of study. He was a renowned popular lecturer on scientific topics, a published botanist, a skilled artist, a doctor on the staff of the new Massachusetts General Hospital, a Harvard professor, an adept amateur architect and landscape designer, and (in what may be his true claim to immortality) the originator of the word *technology*.

You have to go to a rare book room now to view his splendid drawings for a book about New England flowers, *Florula Bostoniensis*, published in 1814 when he was a young man. This resource was not replaced until Asa Gray's work. He had an encyclopedic knowledge of the medical uses of plants (his specialty at Harvard) and was appointed the first Rumford Professor of the Application of Science to the Useful Arts. Bigelow followed that up with helping to found the Massachusetts Institute of Technology.

Bigelow's instinct for reform was part of his generation's hunger for innovation. Creation of the world's first garden cemetery was essentially his idea. Of equal importance was his insight as a medical doctor that the time had come to stop practices such as bloodletting and excessive use of untested drugs, and to let time, nature, and a humble measure of caution take their proper role in healing. His 1835 article, "Discourse on Self-Limited Diseases," was called by Dr. Oliver Wendell Holmes the paper that had "more influence on medical practice in America than any other similar brief treatise."

He was (and there are other figures like him in the founders' generation) a polymath—someone who effortlessly claimed expertise in many fields—and assumed a natural right to exercise his extensive gifts in practical ways that would be unthinkable today. This kind of astonishingly varied career—the Jeffersonian archetype—was essentially lost in a post–Civil War shift to an ideal of streamlined specialization.

The social transition is made manifest in Oliver Wendell Holmes Jr.'s self-conscious turning away from the easy cosmopolitan (in the son's eyes, bordering on glib) excursions of his father, who held a Harvard Medical School post and wrote poetry, humorous essays, and novels. The father was a literary bon vivant and Boston's universal Brahmin figure, but to Holmes Jr.—who was keenly focused on his law career—the combination of his father's varied pursuits was an irritant, something the new America no longer could support. After the Civil War (and to this day) the modern exemplar of the highly focused specialist reigned supreme in the newly industrialized culture. There no longer seems to be a place for people like Holmes *père* or Bigelow (though the eclectic and controversial Buckminster Fuller, who is also buried at Mount Auburn and whom we will see later, comes close to this old ideal). I think this is why such men tend to be lost to history today—they seem consigned to another world.

Bigelow was a tough-minded scientist who extolled the overlooked virtues of decay. He was an artist working not with words so much as with land, buildings, and flora. Mount Auburn, in this sense, is his vast poem entrusted to us. Bigelow's fingerprints are everywhere—he may not have laid out every curve of every roadway and path, or planted each shrub and tree, but wherever it counted, Bigelow left the mark of his influence and inspiration.

The words Bigelow had engraved upon the giant Egyptian Gateway, which was first erected in wood carefully painted to appear as stone, and then recreated permanently in granite, were carefully chosen. They came from the book of Ecclesiastes 12:7: "Then shall the dust return to the earth as it was, and the spirit shall return to God who gave it." Thousands of visitors have looked up to those massive letters and felt that this pastoral setting was nothing less than a theological lesson in landscape. Choosing a devout quote from the somewhat fatalistic book of Ecclesiastes, Bigelow fused biblical words to a paradoxical frame—the huge Egyptian Revival design proclaiming that here, in America, there was every reasonable prospect of eternal life, only you didn't need to be a pharaoh to sample it.

Meanwhile, back in England, something had to change. Wind of a new approach to death was blowing from America, freshening the air and people's daily lives. Mount Auburn had an immediate, powerful effect; new rural, or at least suburban, cemeteries were established based on the Mount Auburn model, and as we have seen, these burial grounds became "improbably, de facto parks."

As in America, people flocked to them to be in the open air, to walk in peace, and to see flowers and swaying trees. The largest was Brookwood in Surrey, with 250,000 graves on two thousand acres. These cemeteries were so successful, and so full of people enjoying themselves, that, as Bryson observes, "gradually, it dawned on the authorities that what was wanted really wasn't cemeteries that were like parks, but parks that were like parks." These were the open areas that Andrew Jackson Downing, and later the young Frederick Law Olmsted, so admired and were inspired by.

The English twin to Bigelow was John Claudius Loudon, a horticultural writer like Downing and a man of wide-ranging interests who had the drive, as well as the vision, to do in London what Bigelow and his colleagues achieved in Boston. He advocated for park-like cemeteries and even predicted the rise of cremation decades before anyone else did. Known for his stern practicality, Loudon also possessed a desire to make every cemetery an uplifting place for all, particularly the poor—"their book of history, their biography, their instructor in architecture and sculpture, their model of taste, and an important source of moral improvement.... Adorn the sepulcher, and the frightful visions which visit the midnight pillow will disappear."

Sadly, Loudon died in 1843 deeply in debt and with his book *On the Laying Out, Planting and Management of Cemeteries and the Improvements of Churchyards* unpublished, but his vision for London won out in the end. In America and in England, these changes were now moving in parallel. Motivated by revulsion at the pitiless common mass burial practices, these reformers were determined that each individual soul was to be respected and venerated by being buried with space, dignity, and even a touch of art. Above all, society as a whole was to be lifted up. Death was getting a new life.

If Bigelow is the father and Brimmer the godfather, then the founder who has mostly been lost is Henry Dearborn. His personal passion to create an innovative scientific garden was the means by which Mount Auburn came into being in the first place. Like a certain Adam before him, he was to find himself exiled.

The original land acquisition, forming the heart of the historic section of the cemetery to this day, was somewhat problematic until George Brimmer bought several farms, bringing the property to the edge of what is now the heavily trafficked Mount Auburn Street. It is here, on a strip of land that runs parallel to the road—where you find the administration building at the juncture of Garden and Elm avenues—

that Dearborn staked out his large experimental garden. The land was bought under the name of the Massachusetts Horticultural Society, and under its auspices the Massachusetts legislature passed a measure creating Mount Auburn Cemetery and Garden as a legal entity in 1831. The thinking was that funds from the sale of cemetery lots would support the garden. It looked, at first, like a marriage made in paradise—a garden whose apple of knowledge was untainted.

As the first monuments were being built, plans for the great new experimental garden proceeded, and Dearborn's first report was idealistic and practical in equal measure. "The Garden also can be very considerably advanced, within the same short period.... The nurseries may be established, the departments for culinary vegetables, fruit, and ornamental trees, shrubs and flowers, laid out and planted, a green-house built, hot-beds formed." He even envisioned that the dredging and deepening of ponds and wetland areas would "afford inexhaustible sources of manure" needed everywhere over the garden. As he and surveyor Alexander Wadsworth began laying out the new avenues of the cemetery and widening old ones created by Brimmer, Dearborn was already transporting from his own nurseries a large collection of healthy, young forest trees, which he distributed along the front of Mount Auburn.

Aaron Sachs, who has done considerable research into the early history of the Massachusetts Horticultural Society, notes that Dearborn exhibited proudly in June 1833 "some beautiful Rose Demi Long radishes." Dearborn proclaimed they were the first foods ever to be grown at a cemetery. He was excited to begin a collection of "vegetable seeds from London and Bombay, apple and plum scions from Montreal." His garden truly was to be a place where every plant and hybrid could be thoroughly tested, a national center for agricultural learning.

Within four years, however, this amicable land and financial trade-off was already breaking down. It was clear, at least to Bigelow and his allies, that income flowing to Mount Auburn from the growing number of interments was the real future of the enterprise, and that the space, energy, and time allotted to the experimental garden was of less interest. In an 1859 annual report, it was retrospectively noted that "in a few years it became apparent that the proposed garden was not likely to be wanted, and in 1835, under an act of Legislature, the Horticultural Society conveyed the whole land known as Mount Auburn to a new Corporation."

The new arrangement provided for a sizable portion of Mount Auburn's income to go annually to the Massachusetts Horticultural Society. This turned out to be a wonderful cash flow for the organization for decades—but the separation did not come without cost. Many of the records have been lost, but even in Bigelow's fairly whitewashed account, anger and a sense of betrayal come through. There is the admission that "the interests of the Horticultural Society and those of the proprietors of the Cemetery lots were not identical." Further, "Considerable warmth of feeling was elicited among the advocates of the two parties; and it became evident that a peaceful arrangement was not likely to be made."

A compromise was finally worked out after "several somewhat excited sessions," and the two parties went their separate ways. The creation of Mount Auburn Cemetery and Garden was seen by all as a great accomplishment, and the tensions were papered over, but it is interesting that Dearborn went on to design another rural cemetery in Boston, the beautiful Forest Hills. The notion of the experimental garden gradually faded away, lost in the annals of its genesis, but as we shall see, Dearborn's vision never completely died and, in fact, has had in our lifetime a remarkable renewal.

Finding Yourself Lost

Many have commented over the generations about Mount Auburn's unique ability to discombobulate visitors and pleasantly turn them around. In *New England Magazine* in 1896, one writer insisted, "Mount Auburn is not a place to be Baedekerized. It is better that the visitor should wander, as I have done, hardly knowing of precisely what he is in quest, and almost stumbling, now and then, upon a familiar name which invites to delay and meditation, than that he should make his way breathlessly along, intent on seeing the utmost in the minimum of time."

Bernard Malamud, author of *The Natural* and many novels that drew from the experience of exile in Jewish life, chose to be buried in the Willow Pond Knoll section with a simple flat granite stone, above the pond. In his late novel, *Dubin's Lives*, Malamud's protagonist is a biographer of Thoreau. We first see him as he follows a well-worn daily path near his home, as if only nature could offer the release he needs from his pain (one wonders if Malamud's fictional ruminations had something to do with his eventual choice to be buried in a place where hundreds walk past his grave every day): "As he hastened on he warned himself to be attentive to what was present, namely nature.... The way to counter forgetting to look was to join up—take courage in having to move your ass off the confining road, be involved." Like a true devotee of the hawk-nosed and odd man of Concord, who bemused and mystified his New England neighbors with his devotion to daily treks, Dubin the biographer follows on. "He wanted nature to teach him—not sure what—perhaps to bring forth the self he sought—defined self, best self?... Now, on the whole, in varying moods Dubin looked at scenery, and scenery, in varying moods, looked at him. If you dared look you earned seeing."

One can walk for hours in Mount Auburn, and frankly, on a fragrant and refulgent (to use a nice Emersonian word) spring day where all is in exuberant display, forget that it is a cemetery at all—though that seems odd and a little unnatural with the thousands of graves surrounding you. But all is so well designed, cared for, nurtured, that even death begins to feel subsumed, quietly tucked away, carved into the countryside with such grace that you realize that your mind has played the most natural, and strange, trick of all: as La Rochefoucauld said in his *Maxims*, "Death and the sun are not to be looked at steadily." The glance of the eye and mind is the glare of beauty as we look, and at the same time, look away. The founders knew this; they counted on it. And they designed it so you might be lost within it.

Since we are Americans and all about self-improvement, I have found Alexandra Horowitz's *On Looking: A Walker's Guide to the Art of Observation* a good companion for the last year of researching this book and for myriad walks through the cemetery. Horowitz is a professor of psychology at Columbia University specializing in cognitive science, and the book is an artful demonstration of what higher levels of observation can achieve when you take as your guide on eleven walks in the same New York neighborhood a wide spectrum of walking companions—a child, a dog, an urban sociologist, an artist, a geologist, a physician, an expert in sound, and more.

Thus, in the last year, I have traversed
Mount Auburn with many guides: a
horticulturist turned administrator,
an advocate for green burials, a
groundskeeper, a landscape
designer, a historian, a
bird expert, a fellow
historian-minister, and
many others, experts
and family and friends
besides. Yes, I have walked alone, but I
felt that going with others would serve to
deepen and enrich my experience, and help me see things I
was not equipped, or ready, to see. William James called the
sensory overload that a baby confronts at birth an "aboriginal
sensible muchness." I needed help in focusing, in narrowing
down, in noticing specifics in the richness.

Most of us are effectively sleepwalking through our days,
and any encouragement to awaken and alert our senses—well,
that is a good. I am adept at many things, but actually *looking
at what I am looking at* as I pass, sadly, is not high on the list. I
have enjoyed researching this book and getting to know the
friendly staff at Mount Auburn—and I have even enjoyed the
writing—but what I am really getting from the experience is
a heightened sense of seeing this place and every other landscape in my life not only with keener senses, but with a willingness to process and notice.

One of my favorite biblical words is the exclamation *Behold!*
You don't have to have an angel whisper it to you. This is what
is being asked of us: *behold.* Unfortunately, it is less a grand
gift than a discipline, and I will have to stretch myself to keep
it up. It will force me, if I stick with it, to see the walks I do
every day, just like Horowitz's New York jaunts, as the means

by which I apprehend the extraordinary in the very ordinary, the "muchness" in the mundane. And it will take more than a place as beautiful as Mount Auburn to make me achieve this (though it certainly helps).

The lost art of walking is often the heart of Thoreau's essential message, as shared in one of his last essays, "Walking," in 1862. In defense of the preservation of wildness, he harkens back to the old word *sauntering*, surely one of the things that Mount Auburn most exemplifies. In the Middle Ages, wanderers would ask for alms saying that they were about the purpose of heading to the Holy Land, "till the children exclaimed, 'There goes a Sainte-Terrer,' a Saunterer, a Holy-Lander." So every walk can become, under sly pretenses perhaps, a pilgrimage, a hike to the Holy Land. Still, striding with purpose or ambling with none, any walk is in the direction of something sacred. "So we saunter toward the Holy Land, till one day the sun shall shine more brightly than ever he has done . . . as warm and serene and golden as on a bankside in autumn," Thoreau concludes.

As long as you are lost in Mount Auburn, let me offer a little advice. Keep moving and the circling roads will not let you be disoriented for too long. They are designed to curl back upon one another, like the spiral in a seashell or the twist in your DNA or the wheeling of the stars above your head (though I trust you'll be out and striding past Story Chapel before they appear). The founders would not let you down. You are supposed to only feel lost, not actually be lost.

And as you go, pay attention. Never let a perambulation in this place be wasted—look up and look around. A lot is happening. A blue heron is gliding overhead. A raccoon is shuffling along the rose hedge to your right. The clouds above you—if you read them right and sense the wind picking up and lifting the silver undersides of the shaking trees—tell you it is going to rain tomorrow. You just passed the grave of the man who invented parcel post delivery.

"You can observe a lot by watching," said Yogi Berra, who said a great many things he probably never said, but you will find it true.

These vistas were designed to confuse you, in a gentle way; so circle on. Turn something off, even if it is just the insistent jabber in your head. You would be surprised how much you will hear when you are silent, and the surrounding air surrenders up its reverberations. It is a good trade-off. Then you can sense the sound of wind moving through tall grasses, and hear the rough caw of an obnoxious blue jay.

Historian Aaron Sachs notes how important these circles and confusing winding paths were to the designers of the cemetery. They were a deliberate turning away from the increasingly grid-like designs of growing vast urban centers. He notes a self-conscious admission in an 1843 guidebook, stating that the thirty miles of paths were "so curved and winding in their course, as to make it difficult for a stranger to keep the even tenor of his way and thread the mazy labyrinth with a mind serene." In other words, this is a peaceful place of nature's solace—except that to fully be in touch with the truth of nature, you should also probably feel pretty lost at times, and even a trifle agitated at that. Sachs concludes, "The cemetery's founders, rather than attempting to commodify and incorporate the natural world, hoped to get lost in it."

Writer Anthony Dorame notes, "Cycles are circles that travel in straight lines. The seasons come in cycles, yet each season marks the passage of another year. We receive our names, plant, harvest, marry, dance, sing, and are buried in concert with the cycles." Yes, the urban designers were laying out Manhattan and Boston's Back Bay in long lines and in tight grids, but other American dreamers were infinitely more attracted to these circling visions, landscapes that were filled with paths and roads following the curves of the ground.

The designers of Mount Auburn instinctively chose these circling and winding roads to define their design at the very same time that the young Ralph Waldo Emerson was writing: "Nature can only be conceived as existing to a universal and not to a particular end; to a universe of ends, and not to one—a work of ecstasy, to be represented by a circular movement." These cycles define more than a landscape, but every life and its contours, and even the cosmos. If these cycles were to be seen in the seasons, they would also be seasons in eternity.

I have come to know the place fairly well, though I still get lost and confused and turned around. Sadly, attaining a sound sense of orientation is not an unalloyed plus. Yes, I can navigate effectively and find that really difficult grave site or locate a particularly glorious view twice in a row, but getting disoriented was part of the joy of the experience, and I am no longer so innocent as that. Sometimes I envy the guy I was two years ago, who was pretty much always lost, because this is a garden that was designed to be a labyrinth.

Even Sachs, as expert in the history and meaning of Mount Auburn as anyone living (outside of the staff), admits, "I have been to Mount Auburn on many occasions, and each time I have gotten lost. Admittedly, I don't try very hard to stay oriented." Now, as a parent with his children trailing behind him, he says this getting lost is "almost magically pleasant, simultaneously relaxing and stimulating." He calls this disorientation "a chastening effect somehow uplifting."

Sachs, an ecological historian who grew up loving Mount Auburn, today lives in Ithaca, New York, where he takes daily walks through another in the long line of rural cemeteries, Mount Repose. As he does so, he wonders why we have, as a culture, largely forgotten the astonishing innovation represented by both. We study the rise of cities, and the effort to preserve huge tracts of endangered wilderness—but we largely forget or overlook those precious spots where our forebears painstakingly and with great creativity eked out a middle ground—quite literally, ground that he calls "Arcadian."

"I find myself stuck on the question of why, with the onset of modernity, places like Mount Auburn Cemetery were obliterated as national icons," he writes, and in his recent book *Arcadian America* (and in a recent academic stay at Harvard) he continues to question whether this tradition of rural public space can be better remembered and used to improve our lives. "Why did the core textbook I assigned in my first U.S. history course not even mention Central Park? In a country whose early nineteenth-century leaders insisted on a pastoral culture, why have we been reduced to choosing between the City and the Wilderness?"

Sachs is asking important questions, and I was glad to encounter him as I asked my own questions about Mount Auburn. He spoke at my church one winter evening on his work in environmental history. When he began his sabbatical year he was feted with a dinner welcoming him to Mount Auburn, and he offered a fresh lecture at the close of his time before returning to his professorship at Cornell. In all these encounters, I sensed his passion for unlocking a fresh and vitally needed perspective on the history of our relationship with nature. As a minister and historian, I was at first more concerned with the people buried and how they were mourned and remembered. I met Sachs just in time to realize my work would be sadly incomplete if I did not reckon with the land, the wildlife, and the founding vision, and—surprising to me—how that vision is extraordinarily important in a time when our relationship with nature has become precarious, even endangered.

Sachs helped me understand that the history of Mount Auburn is still being written and that its greatest service to the republic might well still be ahead. We have to forge a new relationship with nature, one in which a small, nearly urban landscape like Mount Auburn might well have more to do with saving ourselves than do the mammoth acreages of Yosemite and Yellowstone. We need to preserve wilderness, but Sachs's work helps us understand that a place like Mount Auburn can help us save ourselves as we protect the increasingly fragile balance of birds, grasses, trees, water, and air, and the breathing groves of forest.

The lure and splendor of the landscapes of national parks led Sachs to make what feels to me a profound observation: "I have been able to see the wilder side of tamer landscapes." Yes, Mount Auburn is only 175 acres, "but its cultural significance—at its founding and 180 years later—has been vastly underestimated, because its complexity, its diversity, its intensity, all foster a lasting awareness of the inextricability of human society and wild nature."

In other words, if we are to stumble our way into a viable future, we had better pay attention to the survival of places as small as Mount Auburn—or we are cooked. Wilderness areas are duly protected and largely bordered off from the worst we can do (though climate change is the joker in the deck for every inch of the earth), but the fragility and importance of places poised on the border at the changeable hinterland between rural and urban—that is too easily lost and overlooked. It is at precisely such places where we will make our stand, and rise or fall together.

Too rhetorical? The staff at Mount Auburn do not think such assertions are stated lightly or glibly. They are working not simply to preserve historic ground, but to use their responsibilities to demonstrate how the founders' vision may serve to save us in ways the founders could never have envisioned, yet somehow anticipated. In this way, Mount Auburn is a gift, an unexpected and strange relic that is more than an echo of the past, but an evocation of a better future.

When visitors to Mount Auburn write about its luminous quality, its sense of being, as the Irish say, "a thin place," where heaven and earth meet and mingle interfused, I am reminded of an old Middle Eastern story where the great soldier and conqueror Amr Ibn Al-as is asked to describe what it was like to almost die, and he answers, "I felt as if heaven lay close upon the earth and I between the two, breathing through the eye of a needle." I like that. Not "seeing" through the eye of the needle, but breathing—being physically present and being drawn through a space of transition. The great thing about Mount Auburn is that to feel this, you don't actually have to be dying. You just have to walk. It is enough to cross through, and to be present.

Rebecca Solnit's remarkable *A Field Guide to Getting Lost* is a far-ranging exploration of what it means to reorient ourselves to this world, to learn to move through our lives with less a sense of control than with a heightened sense of wonder. She notes Walter Benjamin's observation that to be lost is not the same as losing one's way, whether in a city or in a forest—that it calls "for quite a different schooling."

How different? "To lose yourself: a voluptuous surrender, lost in your arms, lost to the world, utterly immersed in what is present so that its surroundings fade away. In Benjamin's terms, to be lost is to be fully present, and to be fully present is to be capable of being in uncertainty and mystery. And one does not get lost but loses oneself, with the conscious choice, a chosen surrender, a psychic state achievable through geography."

I love that—using "geography" as a means of *not* knowing where you are, and being calm, centered, aware in that wandering, that wondering. I believe this state of surrender is exactly what the founders were designing this landscape for. In our present world, we have a GPS in our car and a smart phone nestled in our pockets, with a satellite overhead in constant contact with the signal we emit as we go. There's no getting lost in that scenario; you can't take a step off the grid.

During a recent brainstorming session I attended on the improvement of visitors' experiences, a well-meaning suggestion arose relating to a new innovation being tested then at the nearby Arnold Arboretum: headphones that give automatic information as you walk through the park, pinged by signals encoded alongside certain trees. A voice in your ear would tell you what kind of tree you just passed. ("I'm a European Beech!") Maybe, like the old car tapes produced for Mount Auburn years ago, we could do the same all over the cemetery, for walkers going through woods . . .

I understood the creativity of the effort, and I am sure there is much information I am missing as I walk through Mount Auburn. But the idea left me deflated. I don't come to this place for information, or even to clearly know where I am. I come to reach that place of a pleasant, freeing unknowingness, and I'm pretty certain that wearing earphones will not help me with that. Earphones certainly won't help me hear the songs of birds.

Solnit reports that Sachs sent her a quote from Thoreau's

Walden after she wrote him inquiring into the experience of early explorers:

> It is a surprising and memorable, as well as valuable, experience to be lost in the woods any time. Not until we are completely lost, or turned around,—for a man needs only to be turned round once with his eyes shut in this world to be lost—do we appreciate the vastness and strangeness of nature. Not till we are lost, in other words, not till we have lost the world, do we begin to find ourselves, and realize where we are and the infinite extent of our relations.

A New Manifestation

Megan Marshall's recent Pulitzer Prize–winning biography of Margaret Fuller ends with the compelling image of Fuller's marble cenotaph. Installed at the Fuller family lot at Mount Auburn in 1845, five years after her tragic death by drowning, the memorial quickly became a place of pilgrimage. "In the years after, so many visitors—grieving, curious, inspired—made their way to Margaret's memorial stone that the route leading directly from the entrance up the hillside to the Fuller plot became a well-worn path and eventually the first paved road in the cemetery."

Though Fuller was always controversial, often perceived as troublesome in her time, few did not recognize that she was a central figure in the roiling reform currents of the young nation, tapping into the energies she called "The New Manifestation." My denomination's hymn book has taken this piece of her writing on the evolving relationship between women and men and made it into a liturgical responsive reading. In these words, her relation to her era is made clear: "We would have every arbitrary barrier thrown down. We would have every path laid open to Woman as freely as Man. Were this done, we believe a divine energy would pervade nature to a degree unknown in the history of former ages. A new manifestation is at hand, a new hou   come."

Yet fifty years ago, this towering Transcendentalist was

almost forgotten. If she were remembered at all, she was dismissed with the usual retelling of an anecdote in which she announced, "I accept the Universe," and Thomas Carlyle replied, "Ye Gads, she'd better!" She was seen as, at best, the hectoring old maid of American letters, the woman whose brain was too prodigious for the comfort of her enemies and friends alike. She once wrote, "I know all the people in America worth knowing, and I find no intellect comparable to my own."

It turns out, after a revolution in reassessment—and in the aftermath of five new biographies, of which Marshall's is the most personal and convincing—that perhaps she wasn't wrong. The man she made most uneasy, Emerson, wrote of her after her death: "She had only to open her mouth and a triumphant success awaited her." As he wrote that, he was likely engaging in wishful thinking. This female gadfly was returning home to America from a sojourn in Europe with a manuscript about the failed rebellion in Rome; with her baby, Nino (suspected by glum New England friends to have been conceived before marriage); and with an Italian count trailing along as her new husband. Would America truly embrace this Byronic woman?

This question was, unfortunately, made moot by her shocking death, as her ship caught on a sandbar in a howling storm, floundered, and sank in Long Island Sound within sight of shore. She clutched her child on the drenched deck, desperately trying to save him, and a crew member, seeing more great waves coming to shatter the ship, grabbed Nino and jumped. Fuller died along with her husband and child in the wild storm, and her body was never recovered—nor was the manuscript, assumed to be her masterpiece, ever found.

It has taken a long time to truly recover her. While she was editing the famous *Dial* magazine that was at the center of the new tempest called Transcendentalism, she gathered Boston women on West Street for what she called "conversations," rare opportunities for them to speak and be heard. Strange that it took so long for her own voice to break through.

She recalled: "From a very early age I have felt that I was not born to the common womanly lot." Sarah Margaret Fuller was born in Cambridgeport, Massachusetts, in 1810, and was given a wide-ranging classical education guided by her father, Timothy Fuller. After becoming a teacher in Bronson Alcott's school, she found herself drawn into the circle of Emerson and his literary disciples. She felt the growing clamor of change all about them needed something; it was missing a woman's voice.

Emerson admired her, and he found her one of the few people in his midst who answered back, sparred with him, challenged him at every turn—even to the point where he admitted he was not capable of offering affection to her as she might wish. When he needed to step back as editor of the *Dial* magazine, she, as the only female in the Transcendental Club, stepped forward as editor and chief contributor.

This was the era when Boston saw itself as the "Athens of America," a time in which a confounding collection of conservative verities and a long and righteous tradition of reform existed together and commingled. This remained true even in Emerson's era, when Unitarianism started to take over from the old Calvinist religion, when it was said that the new faith's adherents believed "in one God, at most." Yet even in this spiritual shift, some things proved stubbornly persistent—a sense that the world was looking on, waiting for the Boston answer to everything.

At times, it seemed that the center of New England thinking was actually Fuller, though this renown seemed to bring her little joy. She was often lonely, and reading her writings today one can sense a painful mixture of self-awareness and true despair. She knew she could publish, she could lead groups, she had influential friends who admired her (some, like Emerson, who preferred to do so from a distance). Yet she needed to seek solace, as so many people did, in the embrace of nature, if not human relationships. She wrote of the comfort of seeing the familiar view of the curving Charles, "the river so slow and mild, the gentle hills, the sunset over Mt. Auburn."

Finally, she decided to cast herself free of her home constraints. Although most writing about Fuller concentrates on her ties to Boston Transcendentalism, it is in the years afterward—when she went to New York to write for Horace Greeley's *New York Tribune* and later when she traveled abroad as America's first woman foreign correspondent—that she found greatness. In this period she wrote *Summer on the Lakes*, her first book, about the healing power of nature, and when, passing through Boston, she once again wrote in her journal: "Spent the afternoon in Mt. Auburn. It was of heavenly beauty."

It got uncomfortable for her again after her notorious feminist tract *Women in the Nineteenth Century* was published, so she decided to travel abroad to cover the rebellion of Rome in 1847. She was drawn into the conflict and found herself directing a hospital, helping wounded freedom fighters. Falling in love, and abandoning her old New England hesitancies, she had a child with a man named Giovanni Angelo, Marquis Ossoli. Even through all this, she kept up a stream of dispatches to New York and kept working on a history of the failed rebellion and on her experiences in the Siege of Rome.

After Fuller completed the manuscript, the couple resolved to return to America. Then, so close to landfall, all three perished. Emerson sent Thoreau to the shores of Long Island to find her body and effects. Except for the body of her baby, Nino, nothing was recovered. The cenotaph for Fuller at

Mount Auburn, where Nino and other members of the Fuller family are buried, is a memorial for one lost. Yet, as with the Colonel Robert Gould Shaw memorial, sometimes the body does not need to be present for a presence to abide.

Emerson wrote to Thomas Carlyle in 1840 that "we are all a little wild here with numberless projects of social reform, not a reading man but has a draft of a new community in his waistcoat pocket." In his survey of the Jacksonian era, *Waking Giant*, David Reynolds estimates that over one hundred thousand Americans were members of some sixty utopian communities in that period.

But you did not have to run off to join the Shakers or the Unitarians at Brook Farm to be a part of social ferment, to add your voice to innumerable reform movements. All of life seemed to be up for improvement, as if it were your birthright as an American to voluntarily join in some effort to insure that the rest of the world saw the United States as a great experiment. Fuller's New Manifestation was reflected everywhere, in every aspect of life, and certainly in the burial of the dead. Mount Auburn can be seen as one small part of a great wave of reform.

When I began this project, one of the first books directed my way was Louis Masur's *1831: Year of Eclipse*, a survey of American life across one pivotal year. Masur focuses on important elements of 1831: Tocqueville's journey across the United States (indeed, to my amazement, Tocqueville's three weeks in Boston would have exactly coincided with the consecration service at Mount Auburn—though there is no trace of the ceremony in the Frenchman's notes); the growing industrialization of New England; the invention of the cotton gin, which turned out to be the salvation of slavery; the

advent of the abolitionist movement, and the subsequent tur-
moil within that movement; the rise of Jacksonian democracy;
and the great solar eclipse. Yet Masur ends his saga with an
event that most historians might have overlooked. He writes
of the consecration of Mount Auburn as an important moment in our cultural life, concluding, "The terror of death
had given way to romance. The fate of all humans was to be
met not with dread but with quietude. Planted in nature and
surrounded by the peaceful solitude of nature, the city of the
dead became a city of eternal life."

Above all, Masur reminds us that this was not a sleepy,
calm, uneventful time. On January 1, 1831, the utopian dreamer
and developer Robert Dale Owen wrote, "Never, perhaps,
since the period when history first speaks to us of the doings of
man, did a year open upon the world that promises to be more
rife with improvements and mighty changes, than that which
commences today. The WORLD is in a state of revolution."

This period is quite possibly the least understood and appreciated era of our history. For us, most of the years from
Francis Scott Key's composition of "The Star-Spangled Ban-
ner" to the firing on Fort Sumter are a near blank. Yet the
antebellum period ranks with the 1920s and the 1960s in terms
of radical change and social disorientation. The Civil War
did not emerge from a quiet, placid time of Americans sip-
ping mint juleps and rocking on their porches—it was an
anguished, testing, and yet hopeful time when everything
seemed open to transformation. Movements were afoot relating to women's rights, temperance, worker's rights, apocalyp-
ticism, sexual freedom and marriage, prison reform, rights of
the mentally ill, care for and education of the deaf and blind,
the rise of new religions, and, most of all, abolitionism—all
of which roiled the body politic and people's personal sense
of well-being.

All these efforts were born from a strong sense that the world could be made better, that society was ripe for change. The creation of the rural cemetery was not, in this sense, some romantic vision, but was a stern effort of reform fully in line with the swirling currents of change. Reynolds concludes, "If the Jacksonian parties shaped America's future, so did the era's outliers—its philosophers, writers, showmen, reformers, cult leaders, and purveyors of panaceas. There were few phenomena in Jacksonian culture that did not have major ripple effects in later American history.... The militant reformers stand out, for they embodied what was perhaps the Jacksonian age's most important lesson: the capacity of American democracy to question itself sharply."

Yet this is not all. After quoting many sources, let me quote from myself:

> What may seem in old tinted photographs and yellowed etchings to have been a quaint and quiet time was anything but, with the advent of quick-paced and unrelenting technological innovation . . . the invention of the rotary printing press, the laying of the transatlantic cable, Morse's telegraph, Whitney's cotton gin, Fulton's steamboat, the quickening pace of the laying of rail road track, increasing locomotive engine power, Cunard Steamers, Singer's sewing machine, and even the advent of the iron plow—all these made the pace of daily life seem to teem with exhilarating transformation. Daniel Webster concluded, "Society is full of excitement." In his autobiography late in the century, Henry Adams remembered his Beacon Hill childhood and his sense that his "old universe was thrown into the ash-heap and a new one created."

At the center of the Beacon Hill reform sensibility was a tiny, shy, almost gaunt man, usually seen scuffling down Mount Vernon Street bound up in multiple layers of coats and scarves, with a great brimmed hat. All of Boston revered him—even those who worked hard against his gentle liberal spirit. Even Emerson, who had grown to dislike the genteel Unitarianism of his own father, saw the Reverend William Ellery Channing as a great man, possibly a saint. Standing before Channing's immense greening monument at Mount Auburn today, I wonder how few visit his burial place now, and how few might even recognize who is depicted in the great sculpture across the street from the Arlington Street subway stop, near the Boston Public Garden. Obscure as Channing is today, he remains a towering spiritual figure in our history, and a man whose influence on so many other reform-minded figures is truly remarkable.

From his pulpit at the Federal Street church, Channing became known as "the conscience of Boston," and though he disliked being involved in disputes, his eloquence and his friendships with reformers drew him into the center of controversy. This was particularly so when, against his inclinations, he helped articulate the central tenets of an emerging Unitarianism—though he maintained that the conservative orthodox ministers left him, not the other way around. His 1819 sermon on "Unitarian Christianity" was the best-selling pamphlet in American history to that time. It made sense that Channing would eventually be buried at Mount Auburn, as so many of the core sensibilities that formed the rural cemetery movement can be traced to his overturning Calvinist theological assumptions. He preached that humanity was not doomed and depraved, but capable of vast improvement, a state he called "Likeness to God."

One by one, all the young reform-minded men and women

came to his study, and he encouraged them to dare to change things, to experiment. This influence extended to Emerson, Theodore Parker, Elizabeth Peabody (who started America's first kindergarten), and Dorothea Dix—who today is buried not far from the man who encouraged her to make a profound change in American life. Again, you may never have heard of her, but of all the people buried at Mount Auburn, Dix may have had as great an impact on pain and suffering in American life as anyone before or since. She found a mentor in Channing, and he helped her survive a long period of illness and depression.

She found, at last, a purpose in life by uncovering the degrading treatment of the insane and the mentally ill. It sounds astonishing, but there was a pervasive belief that those afflicted were incapable of feeling pain. Consequently, they were treated with indifference and near-cruelty. Dix set out, to the annoyance of the medical profession and the state legislature, to visit every jail and almshouse in Massachusetts. For her efforts, she was called a "meddlesome busybody." What she found astonished her: twenty people to a room; sufferers with peeling, diseased skin; rags and stone beds for the ill. She said, "I come as the advocate of the helpless, forgotten, insane … men and women … in cages, closets, cellars, stalls, pens! Chained, naked, beaten with rods, and lashed."

She won her long battle in Massachusetts after Channing's death in 1842, with changed attitudes and new laws to protect people. She then traveled all over the nation, finding in state after state desperate conditions, and leaving behind her decent places of institutional care. Pope Pius IX called Dix "a modern day St. Theresa," and Lincoln named her head of the US Army nurses during the Civil War. She said that Channing had asked her, "What do you intend to do?" The rest of her life was the answer.

One student said to the fifty-year-old Channing, "Sir, you seem to be the only young man I know." He replied, "I hope I am always young for liberty." His inspiring sermons and attractive personality fueled a shift in Boston life—until he hit the tormenting issue of slavery.

As a young man, he had lived for a year in Richmond, Virginia, as a tutor, and he had no animus against the South. Always averse to arousing controversy, Channing was slow to oppose slavery in public, but so revered was he that when he did, he gave needed respectability to the young abolitionist cause. Saying to a friend, "I have been silent too long," he moved to write and speak against slavery—despite the active condemnation of his own congregation, many of whom had shipping and trade connections that profited from the slave trade. The merchants, bankers, and ship owners of State Street resented their minister's willingness to interfere with anything affecting the cotton trade. Even though Channing had once been so respected, some church members crossed the street when they saw him approaching.

After he wrote a book condemning slavery, things grew worse. When his church board refused to allow him to conduct the funeral service for his friend, the fiery abolitionist Charles Follen, he stepped away from his beloved pulpit. He died a year later, in 1842. He had not been defeated; all of Boston soon came to see that a giant had been in their midst.

The New Manifestation that Fuller wrote about was now gathering strength, particularly when it came to abolitionism, with Channing's slow—but in the end sure—encouragement as its core. Yet we miss the truth of that movement if we think that it quickly gathered followers and moral authority until few could argue against the "self-evident" truth that the slaves must be freed. Even in Boston, abolitionism was long a fringe movement considered unduly radical; it was held in suspicion and generated acute social unease. William Lloyd Garrison was nearly killed, threatened with tarring by a mob along Washington Street, and even those sympathetic to antislavery ideals did not necessarily buy into abolitionism, nor did they offer support to agitators whom they saw as a threat to the nation's future, not to mention its bottom line. It took decades of slow change for this small movement to make much headway, and even then it was largely outside events, over which people like Garrison had little control, that caused things eventually to swing in their favor. Abolitionists had little popular support until mass revulsion toward federal marshals and southern slave catchers (who snatched black citizens off the streets of Boston in the mid-1850s), violent convulsions over the Kansas controversy, and—the last straw—the US Supreme Court's *Dred Scott* decision all combined to make Boston at last sympathetic to their cause.

Near the Bigelow Chapel is one of the largest enclosed family lots, containing the remains of the wealthy Lawrence family, many of whom represented the largely Southern-leaning "Lords of the Loom." But among them is Amos Lawrence, whose quote about the sudden shift in Northern sentiment adorns many a history of the time: "We went to bed one night old fashioned, conservative, compromise Union Whigs & waked up stark mad Abolitionists."

At the intersection of Fir and Spruce avenues in the cemetery is a tall, impressive, three-sided marble obelisk, standing in a small triangular lot that commands attention. The monument honors Charles T. Torrey, a young Unitarian minister who died as an antislavery martyr in 1846. Like many buried here, he once possessed fame but is now mostly forgotten.

Torrey, born in Scituate and educated at Yale, was a classic convert to the abolitionist cause. As Torrey's ministry failed, and with his marriage under strain, his convictions drew him toward a dangerous and, for the time, radical turn. The story is now more fully fleshed out in his first biography in over 150 years, *The Martyrdom of Abolitionist Charles Torrey*, published in 2013, and it is a staggeringly sad saga. Author E. Fuller Torrey, a descendant, was curious to know why so few abolitionist histories—even those concentrating on the Underground Railroad, which the young minister died helping to create—mentioned Torrey. The portrait depicts a flawed and desperate idealist who turned from moral persuasion to active (and thoroughly illegal) intervention that, while morally admirable from our vantage point, appears nearly suicidal. Torrey suffered from early signs of tuberculosis. He grew tired of Garrison's nonpolitical form of abolitionism and decided not only to endorse a more robust stance, but to go to the border state of Maryland to run wagonloads of escaping slaves to freedom. Dodging slave catchers and local law authorities, he helped (it is believed) over four hundred blacks to freedom, almost daring anyone to stop his activities. All this, twenty years before the radicalism of John Brown.

Torrey's luck could not last. In 1844 he was arrested and imprisoned in Baltimore to await trial. Even his natural allies despaired of him, claiming he was mad or too ill to be held accountable for his rash actions. His pleas for release were ignored. For two years he hung on, growing sicker by the day, until he at last died, at age thirty-two, in a small, cold Maryland prison cell.

And, as often happens, those who had ignored or even abandoned him suddenly woke up to the usefulness of his martyrdom. His body was taken north, and three thousand people attended his funeral at Tremont Temple. Forty-seven carriages plowed through the rain to his interment at Mount

Auburn. Beautiful bas-reliefs adorn his marble obelisk, and his brief story is enshrined there, but Torrey sank back into obscurity as Garrison's star rose, and his early efforts to establish an effective Underground Railroad were gradually forgotten.

Still, he was one of hundreds of young idealists of his generation who heeded an inner call to combat ills they thought plagued the new nation, that kept it from fulfilling its promise as a beacon of reform for the world. Decades later, a man elected to the presidency on a moderate antislavery ticket (and who expressly denied any connection to abolitionism) would, in the midst of a war few saw coming and yet one that could not be held back, state that the conflict was being fought "for a vast future also." The New Manifestation could not, in the end, be denied. For Fuller, for Channing, for obscure young idealists who threw themselves on the wheel of history, their deaths and reputations were simply energies added to the coming tide.

Words from Torrey's poignant letters from his cell are inscribed on his monument, and they say all one needs to know about these reformers: "It is better to die / in prison / with the peace of God / in our breasts, / than to live in freedom / with / a polluted conscience."

An Earthly Paradise

Seldom commented on is how the theological underpinnings of the New England mind very likely contributed to the creation of Mount Auburn. The key Puritan divine who left the pulpit of Boston, England, to fill that of Boston, Massachusetts Bay Colony, was the Reverend John Cotton, who was clear that the church, and the city formed around the church, was a new Eden "coming up out of the wilderness of the New World as collectively a garden enclosed, 'a Paradise, as if this were the Garden of Eden.'"

This sensibility was so steeped within early New England culture that, even at a later date when liberal Unitarianism held sway, it was a natural motivating concept to draw upon—to make a new kind of holy garden, a place of such delight that death was held in check. It was a movement that seemed to define the whole New England enterprise.

The great church historian George H. Williams is succinct in defining his terms: "The word Paradise, of course, is a Greek adaptation of a Persian word for a magnificent garden. ...In its three appearances in the Old Testament it simply means park." The first garden, Eden, was translated as "delight." After Jesus's time, the word Paradise became associated with that of Heaven—a cosmic garden, if you will. So even if the Puritan spirit in the American mind tends to denote grimness, duty, and repression, in fact they loved gardens and

the beauty of nature. The impulse toward creating Mount
Auburn does not come out of nothing—it proceeds from the
heritage of delight in nature, where even death is absorbed in
the garden of life itself.

Gardens have always figured prominently in founding
myths, and one of the most persistent myths in the Mount
Auburn saga is the belief that Frederick Law Olmsted was
the father of Mount Auburn. Olmsted has accumulated such
fame as America's iconic designer of so many of our greatest
public parks that this assumption is perhaps understandable,
but in fact Mount Auburn's origins predate his active designing career by more than twenty years.

Although Olmsted would spend his final years in Brookline, Massachusetts, and transform the local Boston landscape
with two great achievements—the Arnold Arboretum and the
Emerald Necklace—there is zero indication that Olmsted

was directly influenced by, or even visited, Mount Auburn. However, he did visit it *after* he died, as he was one of the first people cremated in the new Mount Auburn crematory when it was installed. So there is that.

Yet after the Civil War, Olmsted was contacted by the quartermaster general of the US Army, Montgomery Meigs, asking advice on the design of cemeteries for the Union dead. In reply, the landscape designer indicated the chief aim should be "permanent dignity and tranquility"; in fact, all that really would be necessary was an enclosure wall, with trees planted to create a "sacred grove." He indicated the worst thing to do would be to allow anything too elaborate or fancy: "Looking forward several generations, the greater part of all that is artificial at present in the cemeteries must be expected to have either wholly disappeared or to have become inconspicuous and unimportant in the general landscape." Was this a veiled reference to Mount Auburn's second and third generation of elaborate ironwork and increasingly ornate statuary, as the purer and more natural vision of the first founders was beginning to lose sway? The early, darkly wooded glade was getting more jammed with death's markers, and perhaps Olmsted was thinking of more pastoral hillsides for the glorious dead.

In many ways, Olmsted's entire career was made possible by the untimely death of Andrew Jackson Downing in 1852. A protean figure in the development of American landscape design, Downing was our most articulate philosopher of what public parks could mean to our common life, and to democracy itself. While he did not help create Mount Auburn, he is the key figure (though largely forgotten today) in our understanding of how a small rural cemetery outside of Boston could—and did—so profoundly affect the course of public space in our country, from the radical innovation of Central Park, to the designs of Civil War battlefield cemeteries and of suburbs, and, eventually, to the advent of our great national park system. Downing was the visionary who, in observing the thousands of visitors thronging to Mount Auburn, sensed the larger possibilities in creating viable and vibrant common space for all.

As a young man poised between a farming life and a brief but productive spell as a roving journalist, Olmsted met Downing and was encouraged by the more famous writer (although Downing was then only thirty-five himself) to contribute essays to Downing's magazine, the *Horticulturist.* A year later the charismatic Downing, in an attempt to rescue a drowning woman in a steamboat accident, himself drowned. His partner, Calvert Vaux, would later join with Olmsted in submitting a plan for a proposed vast public park in the center of Manhattan. When the two were selected to oversee the creation of Central Park, drawing on Downing's ideas, Olmsted never looked back.

It was Downing, in his influential four books and numerous articles, who maintained that something crucial that he had observed during a trip to Germany was missing from American life—an easy and convivial social intercourse among all classes of people in public avenues and gardens. He thought this was odd in a nation that called itself a republic: "The true policy of republics is to foster the taste of great public libraries, sculpture and picture galleries, parks and gardens, which all may enjoy." Gardens "as great social enjoyments" came first, in his perspective, in this case in democratic mixing—and in moral elevation. A truism in the Romantic age, especially during the rise of Transcendentalist thought, was that exposure to nature's charms would inspire and serve to reveal the soul's true character.

In 1848, in an article called "A Talk about Public Parks and Gardens," Downing posed both as an experienced "traveler" and as an inquiring "editor" who probes why Europe seems more advanced than America in terms of social life. The traveler replies that the difference lies in Europe's "Public Enjoyments, open to all classes of people, provided at public cost, maintained at public expense, and enjoyed daily and hourly by all classes of persons."

The editor asks, "Picture galleries, libraries, and the like, I suppose you allude to?"

The answer is a poetic one, and to readers of Downing's time probably somewhat surprising:

> More especially at the present moment I am thinking of Public Parks and Gardens—those salubrious and wholesome breathing places ... full of really grand and beautiful trees, fresh grass, fountains, and in many cases, rare plants, shrubs, and flowers. Public picture galleries and even libraries are intellectual luxuries; and though we must and will have them as wealth accumulates, yet I look on public parks and gardens, which are great social enjoyments, as naturally coming first.

Later in the essay, the editor asks, somewhat skeptically, what proof the traveler has that such good things are "within the means of our people?"

And this answer is more surprising, but will eventually prove to be a prophecy that will bear much fruit. The answer is found "most of all in the condition of our public cemeteries at the present moment." Twenty years earlier, such rural cemeteries did not exist, now three—Mount Auburn, Green-Wood (Brooklyn), and Laurel Hill (Philadelphia)—were among the most visited, and crowded, spaces in all the United States. "Judging from the crowds of people in carriages and on foot which I find constantly thronging Green-Wood and Mount Auburn, I think it is plain enough how much our citizens of all classes would enjoy public parks on a similar scale." He goes on to add that new public spaces should be built and maintained to reduce in these cemeteries the "gala-day air of recreation they present.... People seem to go there to enjoy themselves and not to indulge in any serious recollection or regrets." In other words, people are enjoying the site—and sight—of death far too lightly!

The next year, he reinforced these ideas in a new essay, "Public Cemeteries and Public Gardens," and he had the figures to support his points. He first lauded Mount Auburn, describing its natural beauty: "No sooner was attention generally roused to the charms of this first American cemetery than the idea took the public mind by storm. Travelers made pilgrimages to the Athens of New England solely to see the realization."

The slight unease revealed in his previous essay is now more clearly stated, but with a more positive angle toward the tide of what we could call tourism. "The great attraction of these cemeteries, to the mass of the community, is not in the fact that they are burial places, or solemn places for meditation for the friends of the deceased, or striking exhibitions of monumental sculpture, though all of these have their influence.... The true secret of the attraction lies in the natural beauty of the sites and in the tasteful and harmonious embellishment of these sites by art." In a footnote that would in a hundred years be fully vindicated (and largely enacted), Downing shows his impeccable good taste by stating that Mount Auburn's beauty did have one flaw: it was "marked by the most violent bad taste; we mean the hideous *ironmongery.*"

Downing estimated that at least sixty thousand visitors had come to Mount Auburn in the previous year, roughly twice as many people as had visited Laurel Hill in Philadelphia. His point was to drive home an idea he would not live to see fulfilled (but which he did, more than any other citizen, to make a possibility through landscape projects that were frankly unimaginable in 1848). "But does not this general interest, manifested in these cemeteries, prove that public gardens, established in a liberal and suitable manner near our large cities, would be equally successful? If 30,000 persons visit a cemetery in a single season, would not a large public garden be equally a matter of curious investigation?"

Jacob Bigelow stands out from the group of Mount Auburn founders when it comes to assessing who is fundamental in its large expanse and wide mission, and we will hardly be able to escape him as we move through this story. But another man is largely lost in the founding myth story, one who actually made it a true garden and whose influence, nearly two hundred years later, is reasserting itself again: General Henry A. S. Dearborn. Emerson wrote of the gardens at Concord, "When I go into a good garden, I think, if it were mine, I should never go out of it. It requires some geometry in the head, to lay it out rightly, and there are many who can enjoy it, to one that can create it." It was Dearborn who truly made it a garden.

Though I love gardens, until I encountered Wade Graham's history of our nation's gardens, *American Eden*, I had never fully considered what gardens meant beyond their surface attractiveness. My feeling for the mission of Mount Auburn was transformed when I realized that gardens are not about plants so much as our feelings about growth—and decay, and then seed time again. A garden is not just something pruned and clipped, it is one of the most socially constructed vistas in our lives. Graham states his work is rooted in his "conviction that our gardens are meaningful—that they say a lot, and that we can read in them stories, not only about their makers, but about ourselves as a people—our people, in Emerson's words: we Americans."

Because we are not dependent on them for either food or profit, a flower garden is social in its meaning, "a miniature Utopia, a diorama of how its makers see themselves and the world." Above all, a garden is a powerful indicator of "the tensions and energies in a constantly changing society." And if the particular garden you are writing about is also a place where the dead are buried, these elements become, I suspect, even more charged.

Yes, gardens reveal a great deal: "political theories, aesthetic preoccupations, scientific and religious ideas, cultural inheritances, and sheer force of personality." Because flower gardens serve little utilitarian purpose, they are extraordinary material, symbolic maps to an inner state. Oddly, Graham says gardens are not especially revealing of our natural environment in its primal sense, "since a garden isn't nature, but rather an entwining of nature and culture in a highly promiscuous, productive pas de deux."

Thus, it is not terribly surprising that Graham centers on Mount Auburn as a prime example of the garden as parkland, as a space of public freedom, of "how a properly executed landscape might lift the spirits in the face of death, and as an investment; it was a success on both counts." Visiting Mount Auburn is a venture into understanding ourselves, what we treasure, what we wish to preserve, what delights us.

None of us may ever make it into paradise, but thanks to visionaries and garden vistas like these, the magnificent horticultural dream that even dour Puritans felt to their bones still operates in American hearts. Andrew Downing never saw Mount Auburn, never stepped onto its grass—but he understood it well as part of our American destiny, our far horizon.

WINTER

I think the moment I realized what made good writing—meaning prose that freezes your mind with awe even as it gives you goosebumps—was when a teacher made us read James Joyce's story "The Dead." I will never forget the final image of snow falling all over Ireland, a symbol of the narrator's leap of awareness of how the dead can claim a loved one's heart more readily than the person in front of them.

These final sentences stun with their internal poetry and assonance, their flow, and their emotionally laden effects. Frankly, every time I enter Mount Auburn in winter, when the land is shrouded with snow and the gray monuments stand out against the undulating white, I think of Joyce's words, and the impossible bar they set: "It was falling softly upon the Bog of Allen and, further westwards, softly falling into the dark mutinous Shannon waves. It was falling too upon every part of the lonely churchyard where Michael Furey lay buried. It lay thickly drifted on the crooked crosses and headstones, on the spears of the little gate, on the barren thorns. His soul swooned slowly as he heard the snow falling faintly through the universe and faintly falling, like the descent of their last end, upon all the living and the dead."

This passage is to prose as Dearborn's design is to landscape, and when winter descends, a new kind of beauty emerges here—more subtle, muted, but stunning all the same. Traces of yellow, red, and purple berries cluster against the backdrop of snow, invitations for the equally bright cardinals to feast in a lean time. Animals burrow deeper into the ground, huddled for warmth and protection from the winds that channel in from the coastline. Easter screech owls stare from their tree hole sanctuaries, surveying the ground for a scurrying morsel, but so much is still, unmoving. Black crows swoop to pick at hidden seeds by Auburn Lake's feeding station, and even their caws hardly disturb the stillness.

This is the time for meditative walks, for moving through vistas that evoke everything Joyce was trying to convey—the sensation that snow here binds the living with the dead in a tight embrace that is unyielding until March is well along, when the first signs of spring pop with the gold-yellow of witch hazel and with the delicate belled snowdrops rising up to anticipate the green force to come.

The grounds crew keeps a special eye out for the fox dens, hoping coyotes—who appear occasionally—will not discover them. These birthing dens are burrowed into sandy soil during the mating time of January. The pups are born in March, and everything possible is done to protect the families while the young mature. It is a great sight to see red foxes darting quickly through the cemetery grounds in the dusk, and to know that another generation is surviving—improbably, only four miles outside of Boston. Rarer still, the sight of weasels and minks, slinking up from the Charles River waterways (where they swim and breed) hunting for muskrats. And the rarest sight of all, the elusive fisher cat.

Sacred Tourists

Emily Dickinson, that most famously reclusive of American writers, seldom left Amherst, Massachusetts. Yet in 1846, at the age of sixteen, she recorded one visit that especially moved her: "Have you ever been to Mount Auburn? If not you can form but slight conception—of the 'City of the Dead.' It seems as if Nature had formed the spot with a distinct idea in view of its being a resting place for her children, where wearied and disappointed they might stretch themselves beneath the spreading cypress and close their eyes."

The young girl's letter, in only a few words, captures the strange power this vast garden landscape, dotted with its growing array of noble obelisks, urns, monuments, and tombs, had on her generation. Only fifteen years after its founding, Mount Auburn had become one of the most visited places in the young republic, and its beguiling power had rapidly transfixed the nation. Mount Auburn was seen as nothing less than an open-air church, a place of moral instruction as well as a horizon between eternities. As wonderful as Mount Auburn is—and I have loved it for forty years—it is hard to believe that it once was, next to Niagara Falls and George Washington's Mount Vernon, America's greatest tourist attraction.

It is estimated that today about 250,000 visitors come each year, so fewer folks visit now than in that era, which only compounds the wonderment. With the much smaller population at that time, the percentage of Americans (along with foreign tourists, such as the future King Edward VII) who felt compelled to visit here beggars belief.

Yet the testimony is clear. A cascade of guidebooks from the period indicated that you really hadn't visited Boston, or New England, or even the East Coast of our burgeoning nation unless Mount Auburn was on your list. John F. Sears, in his book *Sacred Places: American Tourist Attractions in the Nineteenth Century*, tries to explain this astonishing fact by pointing out that there were many institutions that attracted our forebears on vacation that we would not think to visit today.

Yes, Niagara Falls is still on our list, but antebellum Americans flocked to prisons, to insane asylums, to schools for the blind and deaf (and to P. T. Barnum's museum of oddities and freaks). Sears finds that many of these tourists were pilgrims on a kind of spiritual quest, people who believed our country was a kind of special promised land, God's new kingdom. They wanted to see those "tourist attractions (that) suggested transcendent meanings and functioned as the sacred places of nineteenth century American society."

Not only were places like Mount Auburn peaceful, beautiful, and soothing; they were nonsectarian spots that still radiated sacred feeling: "Their religious meaning was broad enough to appeal to people of any persuasion. In a pluralistic society they provided points of mythic and national unity," wrote Sears. We can fairly effectively hide ourselves from the evidence of death in today's world. If you don't want to see a grave, it is not hard to avoid them, and even if you do, they are nicely groomed and mostly tucked away, far from most people's vision. The casket, opened or closed, is less and less present in memorial services and even funerals. More and more, people's cremated remains are scattered along wood paths, in gardens, and on lakes and beaches, with less of a sense of a real corpse having been the origin point of gray dust. We tend more often to die in faraway, antiseptic rooms, where we can be protected from protracted exposure to the process of dying.

Yet there is only so far you can run. As the ancient Greek epitaph reads,

> The way to the underworld is straight
> Whether one starts from Athens or the Nile.
> Don't worry about dying far from home.
> A fair breeze blows from every quarter
> Right to the land of the dead.

In this way, I find the hundreds of people who walk through Mount Auburn every weekend to be amazingly healthy in mind and spirit—in a manner that is equal to the health of their bodies. When asked, these walkers might tell you they are here for the birding, the exercise, the trees, the history. (I don't like to leave until I stumble upon a grave of someone I recognize and didn't realize was a "resident"; most recently I found Marguerite "Missy" LeHand, Franklin Roosevelt's loyal and loving assistant.) But mortality and life's limits press in and compose a subtle background one cannot miss, that cannot be shut out or denied.

A *Harvard Crimson* writer, in 2011, took a Sunday morning walk in October and noted, "The Founders were successful in their efforts. The sunlight dances through orange and yellow leaves. There are no black, crooked tombstones, only monuments of angels and reeds and even the occasional sphinx. Mount Auburn looks like a park covered in sculpture." The author is right: it is a parkland, where graceful sculpture signifies death drained of fear and disgust. Yet no one can possibly walk through unbowed or unmoved. This beauty and these signposts to "the land of the dead" are all inextricably linked, a glorious landscape where the oldest of fair breezes blow in only one direction.

We have already encountered the intrepid English traveler Harriet Martineau at Mount Auburn, but it is important we revisit her because she was a prime, articulate example of what Sears was driving at in terms of Mount Auburn's special appeal. Like Charles Dickens before her, Martineau wanted to see all of America, and though she was shocked and saddened by the oppressive reality of slavery, she visited mostly to see all that was making America a perceived beacon of progress and newness of thought.

She went to prisons and homes for the insane, and to rural cemeteries. She later wrote of her quest: "The idea of traveling in America was first suggested to me by a philanthropist's saying to me, 'whatever else may be true about the Americans, it is certain that they have got at principles of justice and mercy in the treatment of the least happy classes of society which we may be glad to learn from them. I wish you would go and see what they were.' " Go she did, and years later she chose to close her *Retrospect of Western Travel* with a long coda in which she recalled strolling, in the company of Justice Story, the shaded groves of Mount Auburn.

There followed a tidal wave of printed guidebooks, of which, in some sense, the book you hold is an example. In reading them, nearly two hundred years on, the books function like time machines, giving step-by-step tours of a landscape that is to a remarkable degree unchanged in terms of monuments, and yet quite different in terms of feeling. The simple black-and-white etchings bring you back to an earlier time. (The current staff finds these guides important historical documents, and consults them often.) The dense forest of the old Mount Auburn has given way to a brighter, more open atmosphere. Still, a sense of oppression and closeness lingers in the old guides. One reads them with a sense of separation from the fervent and devout religious sensibility in which they are saturated.

Yet there is no denying that, twelve editions in, Nathaniel Dearborn's *A Concise History of, and Guide through Mount Auburn*, demonstrates the strong appeal the place had in early nineteenth-century hearts. The crowds arriving hourly on trolley lines from Cambridge, and the throngs of visitors arriving in carriages and by horseback, all felt they needed guides into this new world, like Dante needing orientation to the underworld in his *Divine Comedy*.

Melissa Banta, consulting curator for Mount Auburn's historical collections (housed in their own, but cheerful, library underworld), writes of these guidebooks, "Together images and text served as a practical roadmap as well as a philosophical and spiritual guide to the garden of graves." The guidebooks sold in the thousands, with authors competing for completeness and deep sentiment. Thank goodness we have them now; they are guides for us still, not only to a historic landscape, but to a lost and seldom-visited terrain of the human heart, circa 1840.

One of the surprise best sellers of recent years is a book first self-published by Lisa Genova, a Boston-area neuroscientist who decided to try to put into fictional terms much of what she saw in real life. She chose as her protagonist a fifty-year-old woman—a Harvard professor no less—diagnosed with early onset Alzheimer's. Alice Howard becomes our guide into the frightening world of a person, prideful of knowledge, who is keenly aware of having it all slowly stripped away.

The novel, *Still Alice*, became against all odds not only a best seller but a recent movie starring Julianne Moore. The movie lost a chance to star Mount Auburn, a significant backdrop to the novel, when it shifted its locale from Harvard to the Columbia campus, trading the autumnal landscape of Massachusetts for New York City's. (Scenes from recent movies such as *Gone Baby Gone*, *R.I.P.D.*, and *Edge of Darkness* have been filmed in the cemetery, so all is not lost.)

In one of the book's pivotal scenes, Alice and her husband, who has not yet been told of her devastating diagnosis, are walking to her family's burial lot on a still January day.

> Today, the cemetery was silent but for the distant tide of traffic beyond the gates. Her crying, explosive and anguished, would have seemed appropriate to any stranger observing the scene—her dead parents and sister buried in the ground, the darkening graveyard, the eerie beech tree. . . . She pictured her own name on the matching headstone next to Anne's. She'd rather die than lose her mind. She looked up to John, his eyes patient, waiting for an answer. How could she tell him she had Alzheimer's disease?

This painful and personal scene is so unlike the ethos that drenches nineteenth-century literature of Mount Auburn and, more generally, of mourning and loss. Here, the place becomes part of her anguish; instead of being portrayed as a source of strength, peace, and solace, Mount Auburn momentarily represents loss and disorientation. There are no answers coming back from the tombstones, no reassurances. This is our modern way.

In an interview in *Sweet Auburn*, the magazine of the Friends of Mount Auburn, Genova describes how she chose the cemetery: "I passed Mount Auburn Cemetery every time I drove into Cambridge or Boston, and I always thought it looked beautiful from my car. *Still Alice* gave me the perfect excuse to actually park my car and look around. I spent a lovely morning there in 2005, walking the grounds, sitting in the shade of the trees, taking notes." Genova's visit was like so many thousands of others, but the result is singular and striking. Her character Alice is a brave and all-too-human guide into loss, and love's tenacity. Having talked with many family members who return year after year to Mount Auburn, I find it remarkable that Genova was so readily able to capture both the beauty, and the desperation, of so many visitors. Not everyone is here to see the birds or trek the hills. Many come to render their hearts of pain, and of thankfulness, too.

The flowers left each day at so many markers testify to the fact that this is no museum; it is an active, vibrant place of family connection.

Though the young Emily Dickinson never returned to Mount Auburn, the memory of her youthful visit obviously stayed with her, as she wrote ruefully of the need for us to enjoy life while we have it:

> When roses cease to bloom, Sir,
> And Violets are done—
> When Bumblebees in solemn flight
> Have passed beyond the Sun—
> The hand that paused to gather
> Upon this Summer's day
> Will idle lie—in Auburn—
> Then take my flowers—pray!

The young girl who so enthused about seeing Mount Auburn and all the sights of Boston would soon enough retreat to her hometown of Amherst and into the confines of her home, and then to her bedroom for the remainder of her short life. But Emily Dickinson continued to see clearly enough the long dimensions of existence, and she captured her visions in short, pithy lines that mostly confused the few who read them. She became, as most nineteenth-century Americans were, very acquainted with death, and she held it with respect and gave it her typical touch of irony:

> Because I could not stop for Death—
> He kindly stopped for me—
> The Carriage held but just Ourselves—
> And Immortality.

The Victorian view of death was so pervasive and persuasive that many of us remain completely convinced this has been the only way those who lived before us ever conceived of an afterlife. The notion that when we die we will then fly upwards to a place called Heaven to experience eternal life is, in fact, a belief that has held sway for only a limited time in Western (even Christian) thought.

It certainly was not the belief of the ancient Greeks and Romans who, at most, believed that death ushered us into an intermediate realm of shadows and shade, sometimes called Hades (but not hell—that notion came later, too), a place where some fading part of our psyches would exist until they slowly dissipated. We might commune with these shades, and they with us, but the message they sent back was dark and despairing—believe us, they cried, there's nothing to look forward to!

Anacreon summed up this sense of the trial of mortality: "Death is too terrible. Frightening are the depths of Hades.

There is no return." Homer has the shade of the great and recently dead warrior Achilles report much the same: "Speak not smoothly of death, I beseech you. . . . Better by far to remain on earth the thrall of another . . . rather than reign sole king in the realm of bodyless phantoms."

The Hebrews for thousands of years essentially shared this stark viewpoint. As Ecclesiastes put it, "Whatsoever thy hand findest to do, do it with all thy might; there is no work, nor device, nor knowledge, nor wisdom, in the grave whither thou goest." Sheol, the Hebrew land of the shade, provides a brief time of transition past dying but little succor or satisfaction— there is no "future" in such a place. It is no heavenly haven.

The Hebrew scriptures give little hope of any true afterlife, other than the comfort of knowing that one's family and, infinitely more important, one's people, provide one's true immortality. God gives life, life is lived, life is surrendered and blessed as the gift it is—it is not a dour or disappointed sensibility, but a restrained and realistic one, and it is summed up well in the fatalistic poetic images of Ecclesiastes 12: "Or ever the silver cord be loosened, or the golden bowl be broken, or the pitcher be broken at the fountain, or the wheel broken at the cistern. Then shall the dust return to the earth as it was: and the spirit shall return unto God who gave it." A life is a vessel for all the joys and trials that fill it, and its materials, and final usefulness, return to the Maker, dust to dust. In this vision, there are no angels or heavenly vistas to be had.

By the time just before Jesus's ministry, there emerges a glimmer of immortality in the book of Daniel, a new note: "And many of them that sleep in the dust of the earth shall awake, some to everlasting life, some to shame and everlasting contempt." But this hope for something resembling an afterlife remains a minority view among Jews. It never truly took hold.

The instinct toward a possible afterlife is more Christian in character, but even there, for hundreds of years, the expectation would be that all believers will be reborn in new spiritual bodies to share in a new Heaven and Earth—and that this could happen at any moment. As the decades, and then the centuries, went by, another vision of life after death took hold—a growing sense that all who die will share in eternal life, in a realm beyond this earthly existence. But this emerging "doctrine" of Heaven was not the belief of Paul or Peter, or of any other early Christians, and possibly not of Jesus himself. This newer "Eternal Life in Heaven" belief evolved and was more fully pictured and populated through the medieval and Reformation mind. It survived the onslaught of Enlightenment reason and reached a high point in the Victorian era.

The early Victorians luxuriated in visions of heavenly gates and glad reunions, of angels playing harps and St. Peter greeting you at the gate—these ideas and images became tightly held and widely shared, and so became wholly a part of funeral rhetoric, art, and custom. It is impossible to "read" Mount Auburn without sensitivity to, if not some sympathy for, this powerful Victorian understanding of death. The dozens of Mount Auburn guidebooks, which offered not only a guide to the emerging landscape of graves but also a vision of Victorian death customs, sought to help the "sacred tourist" make a satisfactory visit.

Doubtless the all-time best-selling book on death (other than the *Tibetan Book of the Dead*) is Jessica Mitford's indignant *The American Way of Death*, published in 1963, and its lessons are hardly less important today, even in a time of rapid shift in death customs. Though the need for its fierce cry against commercialization of burial customs seems perhaps less pressing, it remains a true modern "guidebook" to our new way of handling mortality.

When the book burst on the scene, its author stood proudly in the long tradition of English observers coming to chastise the commercialism and vulgarities of Americans. Mitford responded with anger, and she had her facts in order. It was one of those rare books that really changed things; her indictment of the rising (and ruinously expensive) funeral trade, as well as her searing depiction of the massive Forest Lawn cemetery in California, stands solid today.

Though Mitford's work was nothing like the loving embrace Harriet Martineau gave to Mount Auburn, Mitford is in a real sense Martineau's successor. Mitford notes how the instinct that gave rise to rural cemeteries had, as often happens in America, gotten wildly out of hand. Whereas Mount Auburn had been a place of life—a new Eden—the huge expanses of graves had clearly become a high-pressured industry of death. "There's gold in them thar verdant lawns and splashing fountains, in them mausoleums of rugged strength and beauty, in them distinctive personalized bronze memorials, in them museums and gift shops," she wrote of the new

American cemetery. "The cemetery as a moneymaking proposition is new in this century." In the Victorian period, she added, "charges for graves were nominal, and the burial ground was not expected to show a profit."

Visiting the massive Forest Lawn (the novelist Evelyn Waugh had satirized it in his novel *The Loved One*), she saw with horror where the hyperdriven need for growth (in graves and in profits) had led that old vision of the cemetery as a kind of paradise. The vision of Forest Lawn's founder, Hubert Eaton, in 1917—when he decided to take a small, ragged cemetery and create a vast place "filled with towering trees, sweeping lawns, splashing fountains, singing birds, beautiful statues, cheerful flowers, noble memorial architecture. . . . This is the Builder's Dream; this is the Builder's Creed," does not sound that far from Bigelow's dream.

Yet that dream quickly became more of a nightmare; Eaton was a West Coast anti-Bigelow. He described "a garden that seems next door to Paradise itself, an incredibly beautiful place, a place of infinite loveliness and eternal peace," in rhetoric that is not far from that of Mount Auburn's founders—but the results! The intimacy and warm detail of Mount Auburn contrast with the massive miles of Forest Lawn. Still, Mitford calmly states, "The Memorial-Park idea was born." Whereas Mount Auburn was conceived as a garden, the rampantly commercialized Forest Lawn was fashioned on the model of an entertainment park, as a bright and happy showcase for death in life.

The American Way of Death was meant to be a spear in the side of the undertaker trade. And although Mount Auburn was (and remains) far from deserving treatment similar to Mitford's indictment of Forest Lawn, there is no doubt that her piercing perspective has had a powerful effect on cemetery practices far and wide. It has taken more than fifty years, but, as we shall see, Mitford's reforming "guidebook" to a more humane and respectful way of burying our dead is enjoying a slow triumph, and it is affecting the future of Mount Auburn.

Candles in the Dark

I t is almost Christmas, and the late afternoon traffic out of Boston is increasingly desperate, car lights along Storrow Drive and then Watertown Road out of Cambridge jetted with light spitting snow. Then, somewhat frantically, for I am late, I pull into the cemetery. The lights of Story Chapel give a warm glow against descending dusk, and I hastily park and move quickly, trying to appear calm as I put on my ministerial robes.

Soothing seasonal chamber music greets me as I merge with a long line of people silently moving into the high-arched sanctuary. Each December, people who have recently buried loved ones in Mount Auburn Cemetery are invited to this Candle Lighting Ceremony. Though it is the busiest time of year for all, each year the large chapel is packed, with several hundred souls solemnly filling in the pews, waiting, remembering.

Two local clergy are invited to offer words each year. I speak after Swami Tyagananda, Hindu chaplain of MIT and Harvard, whose smile and gentle demeanor warms the room for everyone. My racing heart calms down and I think more deeply about what needs to be said here this night. I have brought notes, but I find I don't really need them as I rise, go to the pulpit, and look for a moment at the upturned faces. I want them, in this instant, to love this place as I have come to love it. This will not be an easy task, for much pain fills the room, as if the great wooden doors before us cannot quite be shut against that cold, this dread. It is almost Christmas, and they may be here for reasons they may not fully understand, but they have come, and their reason to be here will last the rest of their lives. They are the survivors, witnesses.

So I begin telling them just a little of what I have been learning about Mount Auburn: how they are surrounded by the experience of over ninety-eight thousand other families before them, and how, though this special plot of land is historically important and graced with the graves of some of America's most famous people, tonight demonstrates a powerful truth—that Mount Auburn is not for the famous, not really. Even those who claim some measure of national remembrance are buried here because they were mortal and someone cared enough for them to see them safely here. Each life represented here tonight, and all those who came before, are equally precious.

And I state what I am learning in my research: that each gravestone, famous or not, is in the end a love story. I am not trying to tug at their heartstrings, or manipulate their feelings (which are likely raw enough at Christmas anyway). They are beginning a long process toward learning to know this landscape, in the same way they are learning to traverse the jagged terrain of grief.

It is a simple truth, yet one so easy to lose sight of, especially when we are told by custom that a cemetery is a place of death, of dread—a place to avoid. What I really want to convey is that they are absolutely right to be here this night, and that they should know that they can come here over and over, through every season, at every holiday, each demarcation of the year—all those birthdays, wedding anniversaries—or simply any day to stand and hear the cries of birds, the wind rustling through the trees, silence. I want them to sense how time, memory, and this carefully preserved beauty can serve them well in their passage through and beyond pain.

This pain tonight is palpable, but so is the yearning and expectancy. Nothing the Swami and I can say can be anything more than just an invitation for them to come forward and participate in the heart of tonight's gathering. Carols softly play as hundreds of people leave the pews and place their lighted candles in long lines across the altar and altar rails. As the service ends, they come forward again to reclaim the glowing glass candleholders, and we form long, weaving lines to go out the doors into the arrived darkness and into the great garden named for Asa Gray, the mostly forgotten nineteenth-century botanist who is, not surprisingly, buried here himself with his wife and children not so far away.

Soon large concentric circles of light form along the garden paths, and the staff, as they do every year, leaves them as they are, burning long into the night.

Frozen Transcendentalism

One Saturday morning, some years ago, I wanted to take my son to Mount Auburn and show him Consecration Dell. As so often happens driving around the cemetery, I got somewhat turned around and finally decided, judging by the way I could spy the top of Washington Tower, that I might as well park the car on Palm Avenue and go in by the southeast, a direction by which I had never approached it before.

The woods felt particularly thick and dense that morning. Past Myrtle, and then along Violet Path, we had to sweep the branches away to approach the steep decline. We were now far from well-frequented paths, and the sense of solitariness was nearly total. We passed a few molded old monuments ranged along the upper hill high above the tiny vernal pool, which now came in sight, small, still, and dreaming, rimmed by pale green algae and yellowing lily pads.

As I stood on the ridge, looking down some sixty feet, the sight took my breath away, and I heard my son murmur, "It's so beautiful."

It was. I had never seen the dell in just this way. It seemed as if I had gone back nearly two hundred years and was standing at the heart of another time. Sometimes it pays to get lost, to go by the wrong way.

Though I had been preaching about Emerson and Thoreau for years and had read many books on their generation's

"American Newness," for a moment I stood there simply astonished. Inwardly I breathed, "This is it. This is no doctrine, no abstraction, no metaphor. I am looking at what they believed, and I'm standing in it now." Dozens of times I have been back to the site, but I have never had that sight again.

Long before he left the ministry, long before he published the explosive little book *Nature* that would propel him to fame, Emerson was just one of dozens of romantic-minded Harvard students making their way through the world, drawn to wandering and walking as an expression of their longings, and engaging in wistful rumination on the lessons to be drawn from the woods and the warbles of birds. He wrote in his journal in 1824, remembering his excursions: "In Cambridge there is some wild land called Sweet Auburn upwards of a mile from the Colleges & yet the students will go in bands over a flat sandy road & in summer evenings the woods are full of them. They are so happy they do not know what to do."

Shortly before his death from tuberculosis (when asked if he had thought much about heaven, he had answered, "One world at a time."), Thoreau wrote to a friend, perhaps recalling many walks he had taken at Mount Auburn as a Harvard student: "When the leaves fall, the whole earth is a cemetery pleasant to walk in. I love to wander and muse over them in their graves. Here are no lying nor vain epitaphs. What though you won no lot at Mount Auburn? Your lot is surely cast somewhere in this vast cemetery, which has been consecrated from of old. . . . There is room enough here. The Loosestrife shall bloom and the Huckleberry bird sing over your bones."

These literary men and their circle were obviously well

familiar with Mount Auburn. I have found it difficult to understand the cemetery's origins without reference to their writings, even though they did not create or support Mount Auburn institutionally. Through them, I have found the ability to evoke these generational currents. Transcendentalism is a tough movement to define (or confine), and although I have been a Unitarian Universalist minister for nearly forty years, quoting Emerson and Fuller constantly, it is as hard for me to explain the philosophy as it is for anyone else to do. Transcendentalism possesses a nebulous quality, even for those who admire it, and this certainly is the case for those who continue to dismiss such sentiments as a warmed-over and airy spiritual soufflé.

Over the decades, I have come to resist the usual dismissal—that it was simply a short-lived literary movement of a northeastern urban elite, influenced by the Romantic movement and German philosophical idealism; in the end, pretty much a tempest in a Boston teapot, leaving behind Emerson as its placid oracle and Thoreau as its poster boy. I have come to see it instead as a long and vital tradition, permeating our cultural and spiritual life to this day.

It is represented by figures well beyond antebellum Boston. When I am inspired by poets like Walt Whitman or Conrad Aiken, or by contemporary ones such as Mary Oliver or Gary Snyder, and when I am influenced by writers such as Bill McKibben or Wendell Berry, for me it is impossible to say that somehow the Transcendentalist note was cut off at the Civil War. In fact, its essence seems just as important a sensibility as ever. If Transcendentalism indeed died a long time ago, then our culture certainly could use a resurrection of its core beliefs in this time of ecological distress. As Mark Twain said after a false publication of his obituary—that the news of his death had been greatly exaggerated—perhaps this movement was never quite as dead as many academics and literary historians proclaimed.

Another difficulty is that its very name is a misnomer. What marks the Transcendentalist vision isn't the idea that the world can somehow be "transcended" through murky, elevated rhetorical haze, but rather that, by sensing the very fine particularity of what is in front of us, and *by applying that close observation*, one can realize the pervading divinity within. What is most internal—Soul—is equally present and revealed by the external—Nature. In truth, they are actually one. The world is not forgotten and left behind in our "higher" realizations—it instead stands out clear, apprehended, and fully known.

If the Puritans saw Nature as God's secondary scripture, then Emerson simply made it primary, or rather, one with ultimate truth. The Soul and Nature were interfused. Ultimate reality thus was intimate, not far away or abstract (though putting this particular vision of reality in words of course can make it seem so).

Even in Emerson's own time, people made sport of his early proclamation that "I become a transparent eye-ball. I am nothing. I see all. The currents of the Universal Being circulate through me; I am part or particle of God." His neighbor Nathaniel Hawthorne, aside from having been a genius, remains a compelling writer because he internalized so many striking paradoxes, chief among which (and the central quandary of American life) is the residing strength we draw from our primal Puritan origins and, as well, our simultaneous strong need to reject and escape these origins as best we can.

Hawthorne was no great admirer of his Puritan forebears and the burden of guilt and fear they laid upon succeeding generations, but even so, living among neighboring Transcendentalists, he refused to buy into their optimistic conjoining with Nature's bliss. He tried living their social experiments and listening to their ejaculations of joy and union with the oversoul. In the end, Hawthorne harbored a suspicion that his grim ancestors might well have been wiser and closer to the hard truths of human existence.

His sole "comic" novel was a satirical depiction of the social experiment of Brook Farm. In *The Blithedale Romance* he gives us a sense of what it must have been like hearing the founders of Mount Auburn enthuse on the virtues of their great project. A character speaks of one aspect of creating the utopian community:

> Would it not be well, even before we have absolute need of it, to fix upon a spot for a cemetery? Let us choose the rudest, roughest, most uncultivable spot for Death's garden-ground; and Death shall teach us to beautify it, grave by grave. By our sweet, calm way of dying, and the airy elegance out of which we will shape our funeral rites, and the cheerful allegories which we will model into tombstones, the final scene shall lose its terrors.

A skeptic growls in reply, "That is to say you will die like a Heathen, as you certainly live like one!"

One senses in the thrust of reply that Hawthorne is more than a little sympathetic to that dismissal, that the "airy elegance" of Transcendentalist faith, as well as its attempts to create new institutions, felt at times too elevated and Olympian to satisfy the elemental realities of death.

Although Emerson's "transparent eyeball" moment of insight was not evoked by a walk through Sweet Auburn's rolling hillsides (as a well-meaning minister once mistakenly

informed me), that image sums up the essence of the visionary's task—to sense all that is shining through us, noting how
transparent the world is as we go. This sensibility is, of course,
not easy to attain, and almost impossible to retain. Even calling it the "American Newness" is another misdirection because, of course, seeing the unity of the soul and nature is
an extremely old and venerated idea; it has adherents today
even as it had them long ago. The Greek philosopher Plotinus
spoke last words that demonstrate just how old these ideas
are. He surrendered his life exclaiming, "I am making my last
effort to return that which is divine in me to that which is
divine in the universe."

The old manner of burial—in which a Mozart could be
dumped into a common grave and sprinkled with lime to be
interred with his fellow beings—or for that matter, virtually
any dead body's treatment in the city of Boston until the 1830s,
came to be seen in this reform-minded era as almost a blas-
phemy against this divine self. These new patterns of burial
did not arise solely out of sanitary considerations; society itself was going through a radical reordering of sensibility. The
reforms of Mount Auburn are a key part of this profound
shift, and remain bound up in the Transcendental moment.
Emerson proclaimed it well in 1839, only eight years from the
founding, stating that "ours is a revolutionary age, bringing
man back to consciousness." How one lived, and how one was
treated in death, was part of this revolution in thought and
manners.

Emerson resigned his ministry at Second Church in Boston in 1832, just as Bigelow and Dearborn were completing the
layout of their experimental garden cemetery. Not all were in
favor of a rural cemetery, by any means, because it smacked of

change, of a radical shift that a town like Boston would have to absorb. It was seen as something enlivening and also unnerving. John Quincy Adams wrote of the hubbub over Emerson's newfangled ideas, saying that "after failing in the everyday vocations of Unitarian preacher and schoolmaster, [Emerson] starts a new doctrine of transcendentalism, declares all the old revelations superannuated and worn out, and announces the approach of new revelations and prophecies."

Was Adams thrilled to see all this? The crusty old man would lead the charge against slavery in the House of Representatives after his one-term presidency, yet his comments reveal why Emerson and his many reforming cohorts offered such a challenge to American life: "Garrison and the non-resistant Abolitionists, Brownson and the Marat democrats, phrenology and animal magnetism, all come in, furnishing each some plausible rascality as an ingredient for the bubbling cauldron of religion and politics." All these reforms and upheavals of the old forms left even progressive spirits with their heads spinning.

Mount Auburn today looks peaceful, but it was once very much a part of the "bubbling cauldron" of change, a radical departure from the way life within living memory had been lived. In this sense, it always was, from its beginning, a lively place. Emerson was in the flow of this change, and although he never served the institution of Mount Auburn, his influence was vast. It is truer to say that the impulses that created Mount Auburn flowed into the Transcendental movement, rather than vice versa, but it is also fair to say that the creative ferment of this moment provided the fledgling effort all the energy it needed to be the success and the national model it became. New understandings helped form the spirit of change, riding the wave until they quickly transcended "plausible rascality" to attain respectability.

Alfred Kazin sees Emerson as a protean figure because the writer so effectively taps into this instinct, and Kazin notes that we cannot read Emerson today "without sharing his thrill that in this great, intelligent, sensual, and avaricious America, 'glad to the brink of fear,' he recognized in himself a vessel of the Holy Spirit." It was, Kazin asserts, "the primacy that he shared with Nature and America itself. . . . America itself was the original. The confrontation with it by even the most seasoned men—explorers, missionaries, worldly philosophers and cynics—made things new." When the founders of Mount Auburn called their enterprise "a new Eden," they were tapping into this sense that, in America, all things could be made new.

Even death. And it is at Mount Auburn today where you can touch this sensibility, where its essence has been distilled, made material.

This is the longest quotation in this book; I tried to shorten it, but it is the measure of Emerson's skill as a journal writer that I could not. So here it is, one day's walk through a cemetery only three years old, perhaps an afternoon when American literature changed forever:

> Went yesterday to Cambridge and spent most of the day at Mount Auburn; got my luncheon at Fresh Pond, and went back again to the woods. After much wandering and seeing many things, four snakes gliding up and down a hollow for no purpose that I could see—not to eat, not for love, but only gliding; then a whole bed of *Hepatica triloba*, cousins of the Anemone, all blue and beautiful, but constrained by niggard nature to wear their last year's faded jacket of leaves; then a black-capped titmouse, who came upon a tree, and when I would know his name, sang Chick-a-dee-dee; then a far-off tree full of clamorous birds, I know not what, but might hear them half a mile. I forsook the tombs, and found a sunny hollow where the east wind did not blow, and lay down against the side of a tree to most happy beholdings. At least I opened my eyes and let what would pass through them into the soul. I saw no more my relation, how near and petty, to Cambridge or Boston; I heeded no more what minute or hour our Massachusetts clocks might indicate—I saw only the noble earth on which I was born, with the great star which warms and enlightens it. I saw the clouds that hang their significant drapery over us. It was Day—that was all Heaven said. The pines glittered with their innumerable green needles in the light, and seemed to challenge me to read their riddle. The drab oak-leaves of the last year turned their little

somersets and lay still again. And the wind bustled high overhead in the forest top. This gay and grand architecture, from the vault to the moss and lichen on which I lay,—who shall explain to me the laws of its proportions and adornments?

Maybe you are like me and your eye has a tendency to skip over long italicized quotes; they make your head hurt a little. But go back, try it again, this passage from a thirty-one-year-old widower and retired minister who was only beginning to sense his life's true work. Some have suggested that this passage marked the point, on April 11, 1834, when Emerson had a specific vision that translated into the doctrine of Transcendentalism.

That claims too much, because his insight came not from any specific moment, but from an inner sensibility built up over years. Yet what I find so compelling in this passage is his mode of perception, the specifics of Mount Auburn as a place of *noticing*—and then his move to forsake "the tombs"—then higher vistas of sight that still "seemed to challenge me to read their riddle."

This is a mystical experience that is born out of a walk in a specific garden dell—just one day in the sun, supremely alone and indulgently indolent, a free man who notices things.

What makes Emerson a fascinating figure is the way he moved through life circumstances that would crush other men into numbness. Though Emerson chose to be buried in his hometown's Sleepy Hollow Cemetery, he has an overlooked, intimate connection to Mount Auburn which for me opens up this visionary passage. His first wife, Ellen, died after a short but loving marriage and is buried at Mount Auburn (but she was not interred there by her family until 1878). We know that one year after Ellen's death the young widower went to have her coffin reopened, so he could gaze upon her. That generation's relationship with death is so unfathomably different from ours—we avert our gaze; they sought an engagement that is almost frightening today.

Thus, Emerson's cemetery journal entry, written just three years after losing Ellen, might seem like lofty rhetoric to you, but for me it's absolutely grounded and precise.

He gives us not so much his experience as a path, a process, for us to follow. He shows us a way of perception, with few conclusions. It is all bound up in a short, minimalistic assertion you might have overlooked (I did, too, at first): "It was Day—that was all Heaven said." That is all Heaven ever seems to give us—one day, this day.

The Rivals

With Paul Walker, Mount Auburn superintendent of grounds, we walk to the stately Asa Gray Garden, which you will find immediately on the right as you enter. We had been talking for over an hour in the nearby administration building, but talking about nature is far from experiencing it, so Walker suggests we look at the historic garden, which is tucked down a bit, so that when you walk around the circle path that encloses it you feel far from the busy traffic of Mount Auburn Street nearby.

It is one of the loveliest places on the grounds, with a rounded quadrant garden surrounded by large well-aged temple-like family tombs. In terms of garden design, no location at Mount Auburn has gone through as many changes; for a hundred years, this central jewel of a garden has undergone many rethinks and revisions.

"It's hard to describe how much change this circular garden has gone through during the past decades, but we work hard to get it right; it's such an important spot here. It was beginning to feel old and tired," says Walker as he surveys the enclosed garden. At the founding, it was a pond area, but by 1850 it was converted into an ornate ornamental area called the Lawn, adorned with a large fountain. In the 1930s it was redesigned again, and then once again after it was named for famed Harvard botanist Asa Gray. One way or the other, it has always been a horticultural showcase.

The groundskeepers are implementing a new design from 2000, with more magnolias and new plantings of both Asian and American trees and shrubs, a direct salute to the daring—and at the time socially radical—insights of Gray. And that is not all the recent change. In 1999, past president Bill Clendaniel was told that four large and healthy Japanese maples, each weighing five tons, were a problem in the renovation of the courtyard of the Boston Public Library. Clendaniel responded, "We collect trees."

It was going to be an expensive operation, but forty thousand dollars was quickly collected, and the four huge maples had a new home. They were lifted by crane the equivalent of six stories from the courtyard, and then carefully replanted here in the Asa Gray Garden, where they fit the scene and the refurbishment scheme. On the website of Mount Auburn, it is recorded that the date of the transfer was November 12, Gray's birth date.

In his early defense of Charles Darwin's theory of evolution, Gray, who is buried at Mount Auburn in his wife's family plot, noted that although the Asian and American continents had eons ago drifted apart, there were still clear connections between plants that had continued to evolve separately. These plants, now adorning the present garden as a salute to Gray's keen insight, clearly show signs of common origin. Darwin had creatively used finches and barnacles to convey to a skeptical world that species indeed evolved, and the English scientist was delighted—and relieved—that his American friend Gray was able to bring botany into play as part of a clinching argument.

"These yew trees, these annuals, all the new plantings—in

a sense they illustrate Gray's ideas perfectly, and also provide a new centerpiece for visitors. They show divergence, and also the great similarities," says Walker. The number of visitors who would pick up on such a tribute seemed minuscule to me, but this spot is a proper starting point for the story of Gray and his epic battle with fellow Harvard professor Louis Agassiz. Both are buried here, not far from one another, yet their battle over Darwin's ideas, angry and hurtful to both, still echoes in our national life even today. The plants here tell a tale, and it is of an important turning point in American culture.

The 1860s marked a powerful psychological divide for America—involving more than the shattering violence of the Civil War, the release of nine million enslaved citizens, or the construction of a truly transcontinental railway—that shifted hearts and minds unexpectedly. As well, one important and overarching event—the 1859 publication of Charles Darwin's *Origin of Species*—seemed to change everything. Not only did it instantly transform scientific endeavors from biology to botany, but it had a lasting impact (and occasionally wreaked havoc) on theology, social thought, and even politics. What Copernicus was to the stars, and Einstein to the universe, Darwin was to biology—the cause of a profound shift in which life was seen in a new, and sometimes disorienting, way.

The theory of evolution was so revolutionary that, in America, orthodox evangelicals as well as some radically minded Transcendentalists resisted it. But Gray, the Fisher Professor of Botanical Sciences at Harvard and a professed Christian believer, saw immediately that whatever Darwin's disturbing impact might be, the English scientist was simply offering a new truth and that, at least for Gray, evolution need not inevitably conflict with faith. In this, he was actively opposed by a fellow Harvard scientist with a great deal more clout, fame, and social cachet, Louis Agassiz.

The dispute looked to be an unfair match. Although he had come to Harvard long before the Swiss immigrant Agassiz, Gray was younger. He was a mild-mannered teacher, respected but fairly obscure, and certainly not internationally famous. His rival Agassiz most certainly was, with a great booming, exuberant personality to match that fame. Born in 1810 near Utica, New York, Gray trained as a medical doctor and, like Jacob Bigelow before him, had decided that botany was to be his true vocation. After publishing numerous books and traveling the world for research, he came to Cambridge in 1842, a time when Harvard University had no botanical library or herbarium and only the smallest of gardens. He would change all that in the decades to come. Gray dedicated his first botanical report to "Jacob Bigelow, M.D. . . . Professor of Materia Medica in Harvard University; Author of the Flora Bostoniensis." He settled in and started to work.

Still, despite having earned the respect of his peers, Gray must have been shocked when the thirty-nine-year-old Agassiz arrived at Harvard in 1846 and immediately became—and there is no other word for it—a celebrity. Agassiz came renowned as the chief exporter of the new ice ages theory, which had captivated the world and opened new vistas in recorded time. It was as if he could see the tidal coming and going of the great European glaciers. The Swiss scientist, on tour, had not come to stay permanently in America, but his reception was so welcoming, and the impression that his charming chalk lectures left behind so overwhelming, that Harvard opened its arms to him instantly.

Soon, Agassiz was close friends with Longfellow, Holmes, Lowell, and Emerson, offering a kind of scientific counterpoint to Transcendentalism. Gray was for some years a pleasant enough colleague, though he was struck, not favorably, with Agassiz's definition of a species as being "a thought of the Creator." Gray was a religious man, but that definition seemed simplistic and hardly scientific to him. Agassiz came speaking of "separate creation" as the key to all life, and he would stick to this idea the rest of his life, despite new information. It was less a scientific theory than a lecture hall thesis fused to sermon.

By the mid-1850s, Darwin's frequent letters to Gray outlining his ideas portended a coming great war in the life sciences. Gray was sympathetic to his English friend, and warned him of an inevitable coming battle with Agassiz, who by then was the most renowned scientist in America. In his own inner reluctance to publish, Darwin had delayed for many years confronting the world with his new theory. When *On the Origin of Species* was finally published in 1859, Agassiz moved quickly; he was among the first to ridicule and condemn the book. To Gray, the Swiss colleague said of Darwin's book, "It is poor— very poor!" To a mutual friend, Gray reflected that Agassiz "growls over it, like a well-cudgelled dog—is very annoyed by it—to our great delight—and I do not wonder at it."

Despite these comments from the prominent Agassiz, Gray was moving on several fronts to do the unlikely: make America a fertile ground for Darwin's challenging ideas. Gray helped arrange a new American edition of the book, counteracting a pirated one; he published articles in the *American Journal of Science and Arts* and the *Proceedings of the American Academy*; and, most importantly, he went beyond scientific journals in an effort to sway everyday readers with three powerful articles in the *Atlantic Monthly*. (They would later be part of Gray's bestselling book *Darwinia*.) Gray described his rival "as a kind of demagogue" and as someone who "always talks to the rabble," but Gray did not avoid the conflict in the sphere of public opinion.

Agassiz was not without his own allies and friends willing to edge into the fight. Francis Bowen, Harvard professor of philosophy, immediately published a scathing review in the *North American Review*. Although Darwin's first book kept very far away from any reflection upon human evolution, Bowen's review said, "Mr. Darwin boldly traces out the genealogy of man, and affirms the monkey as his brother—and the horse his cousin, and the oyster his remote ancestor." These arguments are still potent in American life. Yet as strongly held as these views are, they are more emotive than scientific—and to the great surprise of Agassiz and the scientific establishment of the time, abuse and ridicule did not carry the day. Darwin's finches and Gray's Japanese plants did.

By 1864, it was already becoming apparent that, despite the more renowned man's fame, Gray was gaining the ascendancy. Gray's biographer puts their dispute in more personal terms, describing the men riding home on a train to Cambridge from a scientific meeting in New Haven: "There 'the controversy was continued with such acrimony that Professor Agassiz made an end of it by calling Dr. Gray "no gentleman." ' . . . In Gray's code, to call him no gentleman was sufficient to insult him 'foolishly and grossly.' " Apparently there was no truth in the rumor that the European challenged the American to a continental duel—but tempers were high enough.

The years that followed and the tidal wave of approval for Darwin's work settled the arguments within scientific circles, and the two men continued their impressive respective work. Gray became the dean of American botany, while Agassiz founded the Harvard Museum of Comparative Zoology, still a scintillating temple of American science. They managed to stay out of each other's way in Cambridge, which was, in those days, more a village than a city.

They were buried with honor at Mount Auburn, Agassiz in 1873 and Gray in 1886. James Russell Lowell wrote of Gray:

> Just fate: prolong his life, well spent,
> Whose indefatigable hours
> Have been as gaily innocent
> And fragrant as his flowers.

As is often the case, the one who was on the right side of history eased in time into a gentle and honorable obscurity. I found it rather hard to find Gray's grave, which is in the Loring lot of his wife's family, under the overarching branches of a tree that shadows the spot. The burial place for Louis Agassiz and his renowned wife, Elizabeth Cary Agassiz (remembered as the first president of Radcliffe College) is prominent and quite easy to find. It's hard to miss a massive 2,500-pound boulder from the terminal moraine of a great Alp glacier that proclaims, in effect: here lies the man who discovered the flowing eons of the ice ages.

It is an impressive monument for an impressive man, one who was well loved and respected, and who can still be called the creator of modern American science. His more than four hundred books are still consulted and, though he was beaten back on the Darwin front (hardly a minor defeat), he remained for decades the very lively and energetic epitome of the scientist in our emerging technological culture.

Ironically, it was his attraction to the Romanticism of his close Transcendentalist friends that led him astray on the dispute that mattered most. Gray was the Christian, Agassiz the less orthodox believer, but one man believed fervently that the Creator moved in straight lines in making life upon the earth—once created, always created. And this belief lead Agassiz to his greatest misstep of all, not in resisting Darwin but in falling prey to the rigidity of the concept of race. It seems almost impossible to imagine a nineteenth-century scientist making the front pages of a recent edition of the *New York Times*, but the discovery of Agassiz's "racial" photographs—taken to prove the immutability of the so-called races of humanity—achieved this dubious goal several years ago.

Louis Agassiz awed America with his scientific prowess and his ability to convey his wide-ranging enthusiasms. He has been forgiven for refusing to credit Darwin's theory of evolution, which he fought to his dying day. Now, sadly, he is mostly remembered for his rigid racial theories. His belief in the inferiority of blacks remains a potent and still-painful reminder that the energies of the young republic could be misdirected.

Nevertheless, Agassiz willingly gave his life to promoting the scientific method, and to the founding of the Harvard Museum of Comparative Zoology. He was incorrect, but he taught a young nation how to revere a process, and he established a place of research where his fondest beliefs would later be found, through trial and error, to be profoundly wrong.

The Poet and the Abolitionist

Mount Auburn is full of poets—it's a forested American version of Westminster Abbey's Poets' Corner. This is a landscape that rhymes. It is said that more than forty renowned poets rest here, and that is not hard to believe. On Tulip Path you can find the Creeley family lot, where generations of this old New England family quietly lay. One more of the clan has joined their company, with the death of poet Robert Creeley, in 2005. He wrote a calm, subdued poem about visiting his future grave site, in which he describes the "Point of hill / we'd come to, small / rise here." He notices the path names as he, after feeling a bit lost, finally comes to his family plot, located on "that insistent / rise to heaven." The family names come to him as well: "Charlotte, Sarah / Thomas, Annie / and all."

Creeley's wife, Penelope, later wrote to the Mount Auburn staff about that day and about Creeley's deep love for the spot:

> His sense of connection to Mount Auburn was as intricate as his connection to his family, and to New England. . . . Robert felt a kinship here, with the people, with the trees, with the roll of the land, the changes of light and weather. . . . In life he loved "the company," as he called his friends, fellow poets and beloveds, and liked the idea of sharing some of the

same company in death, too. "with / wave of hand I'd / wanted them one / way or other to / come, go with them."

The poet and his wife strolled through the fall afternoon, "in shafting golden sunlight and blazing leaves," and then Creeley fell silent. "I asked him if he felt sad, or spooked.

"'Oh, no,' he said, 'not at all. I feel comforted. It's very reassuring. I'm home.'"

It is a rare visitor to Mount Auburn who does not instinctively turn left after the Story Chapel area and walk along a high point called Indian Ridge, a geological artifact known as an esker. The ridge was left by an ice floe stalled eons ago in the retreat of the last of many repeated ice ages. Soon enough, the visitor will be standing at the Longfellow family plot, where the poet sleeps along alongside two wives and four children.

As a young man, Longfellow strolled over to the six-year-old cemetery to view his new purchase, this plot of ground. There he buried his first wife, Mary, who had died in childbirth while they were traveling in Europe. He wrote, little dreaming of the later tragic death by fire of his second wife, Fanny: "Yesterday I was at Mount Auburn, and saw my own grave dug; that is, my own tomb. I assure you, I looked quietly down into it, without one feeling of dread. It is a beautiful spot."

Literary critics tell us that Longfellow is hardly worth reading today, a "fireside poet," much too safe and sentimental for the rigors of modern poetry. One critic wrote in 1932, "Who, except wretched schoolchildren, now reads Longfellow? ... To minds concerned with the imaginative interpretation of man, of nature and of human life, Longfellow has nothing to say." Since then, things have not gotten much better for his reputation, with fellow poet Howard Nemerov grudgingly seeing Longfellow as "stretching a relatively small gift over a very large frame."

Someone has forgotten to tell that to the hundreds of visitors every month who come to his grave and flock to his nearby home on Brattle Street. Perhaps the academics are right and no one reads him, but strangely, everyone remembers him.

At the beginning of World War II, Winston Churchill took to the airwaves to read to his beleaguered people a letter he had just received from FDR, in which the president had handwritten a verse from Longfellow:

Sail on, O Ship of State!
Sail on, O Union, strong and great!
Humanity with all its fears,
With all the hopes of future years,
Is hanging breathless on thy fate!

The prime minister shared these words not merely to offer a morale boost to his listeners, but to imply that America would not forever stand idly by as Hitler progressed, that this ship of state would somehow, at some propitious time, sail to their rescue—that they were not alone as they faced the future. FDR knew the power of Longfellow's poem, and so, alertly, did Churchill. (Lincoln, hearing the poem recited during the Civil War, remarked with tears, "It is a wonderful thing to be able to stir men like that.")

"Paul Revere's Ride," published in 1861, is one of the few poems American children still recognize. (Actually, without Longfellow, few would even remember the real Mr. Revere.) The work is a focus of renewed interest among scholars re-evaluating its meaning in the context of Longfellow's aboli-

tionist leanings. As the Union stumbled into a long conflict with the South—a conflict it apparently was not ready for—"Paul Revere's Ride" quickly became a bracing tonic for the public, reminding it of all the qualities it took to stand for liberty.

In his later years, Longfellow held a literary soirée of close friends to respond to his innovative and, for its time, daring translation of Dante's *The Divine Comedy*. This gathering became the basis of the best-selling thriller *The Dante Club*, in which the poet's friends band together to catch a serial murderer who, it seems, is a little too attached to the literary horrors of *The Inferno*. It may be hard to believe now, but few Americans had read Dante before Longfellow taught it at Harvard. In this and in other translations, he was breaking new ground in bringing world poetry to a curious public. His mastery of nine languages made him the key figure bridging European culture and our own. Yes, his own poetry was wildly popular, but it was Longfellow—no matter the fate of his own poems in today's literary canon—who opened for us an awareness of world literature.

Longfellow's poetic strengths may have been misperceived even in his own time. In poems such as "The Courtship of Miles Standish," "The Song of Hiawatha," and the heart-breaking "Evangeline" (the basis for one of the last great songs recorded by The Band), Longfellow acted less as a lyric poet than as an ancient figure—the bard, a storyteller for a new nation that had little deep cultural tradition to draw upon. Almost single-handedly, he provided it. When modern critics dismiss Longfellow, they overlook his greatest literary contribution—fashioning national myth. From the ride of Paul Revere to the exile of Evangeline, these mythic tales spun out of American life made him the man who helped the world see the young nation on equal literary terms. It was no coincidence that he was the first American to be commemorated in Westminster Abbey's Poets' Corner.

For Longfellow, things tended to move slowly—he was long a renter at Craigie House, Washington's home during the siege of Boston before it became his; his beloved Fanny Appleton seemed to take forever to decide to marry him (happily, despite her earlier mockery of him); and his transition from weary language professor at Harvard to full-time poet took longer than he wished—though he was a trendsetter in this role, as few Americans before him earned livings as writers of creative verse or prose. Still, by 1854 he was nationally renowned and free to write, a doting father to five children, married to the woman he adored. Oliver Wendell Holmes once wrote that he trembled when he passed the happy Craigie House, thinking that Longfellow's great good fortune could not last. The poet was surrounded by good friends, including Holmes, Samuel Gridley Howe, Cornelius Felton, and, closest of all, the handsome and socially awkward Charles Sumner, the new senator from Massachusetts, who passionately shared his antislavery views.

Then, in 1861, disaster struck. On a hot July afternoon, Fanny was sealing a lock of one of her children's hair with wax when a touch of flame set her summer dress afire. She ran to Longfellow, who threw a small rug over her and hugged her tightly to snuff out the fire, burning himself, but to no avail. She was taken upstairs, where she died the next morning. She was buried along with Mary, his first wife, and a child who had died years before, also named Fanny. Still recovering, Longfellow did not attend the funeral or burial, and after he healed he kept a long flowing white beard to cover his scars, the image by which we recall him today. But scars never really heal. For those who maintain that Longfellow is a shallow poet, perhaps they have never read his lament for Fanny, unpublished in his lifetime:

> There is a mountain in the distant West
> That, sun-defying, in its deep ravines
> Displays a cross of snow upon its side.
> Such is the cross I wear upon my breast
> These eighteen years, through all the changing scenes
> And seasons, changeless since the day she died.

As if that burden of grief were not enough, his restless and somewhat aimless son Charley signed up to fight for the Union. Soon enough, Longfellow received the heart-stopping news that Charley had been shot in the back, the bullet just missing his spine. Luckily, after rushing to Washington, DC, to see Charley, Longfellow was able to bring him home to Cambridge for a long recovery. As Longfellow anxiously nursed his son, he drew upon the experience to write "I Heard the Bells on Christmas Day." Two verses, rarely sung, constitute the heart of the piece:

> Then from each black, accursed mouth
> The cannon thundered in the South,
> And with the sound
> The carols drowned
> Of peace on earth, good will to men!
>
> And in despair I bowed my head,
> "There is no peace on earth," I said,
> "For hate is strong,
> And mocks the song
> Of peace on earth, good will to men!"

The poem's sense of wartime despair makes it an unlikely candidate to become a popular Christmas carol, but when people sing it today there is a bracing sense of triumph in the closing affirmation of the angel's song:

> Then pealed the bells more loud and deep:
> "God is not dead, nor doth He sleep!"
> The Wrong shall fail,
> The Right prevail,
> With peace on earth, good will to men!

He continued to write poetry until he died. His last lines read: "The world rolls into light / It is daybreak everywhere."

Emerson was present at Longfellow's funeral, in 1882, though he was slipping into a gentle dementia. Turning to his daughter, he said, "I cannot recall the name of our friend, but he was a good man."

Every poet, every writer, wonders if her name will survive longer than her last breath and the wearing away of her name chiseled on marble—if any of her work will somehow survive. In his journal three years before his death, the already legendary poet recorded an amusing exchange. As Longfellow stood in the doorway of his iconic home, a lady approached and asked if Longfellow had been born there. He answered no. She paused, then asked, "Did he die here?"

"Not yet," Longfellow replied. Not yet.

Winding its way into Mount Auburn, the funeral procession for longtime Massachusetts senator Charles Sumner was the longest in the cemetery's history. True, the senator could be humorless and a bit pompous, and incendiary when it came to condemning his enemies (one of whom beat him senseless on the floor of Congress)—but he was loved because he stood steadfast for something powerful: equality. He said—when it was not popular or convenient—that black men and women were in fact full citizens and, despite slavery's curse, always had been.

He pushed for this simple idea before, during, and after the war. Although many of his congressional bills proclaiming this assertion were defeated and often derided, he was victorious when it counted most, notably in his sure support for and friendship with Lincoln.

The senator pushed and prodded the seemingly slow president to make an end to slavery the true purpose of the great war, rather than the mere preservation of the Union. Yet when other Radical Republicans and abolitionists criticized Lincoln for being reluctant and always late, it was Sumner who defended Lincoln, saying that while the president seemed to be always six months behind, it was only because he was making certain "the people" were catching up. And in the case of the Emancipation Proclamation, Lincoln was in fact ahead of Sumner.

For all Sumner's education, erudition, and sophistication, he finally realized the Illinois lawyer, whom he had originally thought a rural bumpkin, was actually a more effective antislavery advocate than himself. Certainly, Lincoln's wily and sure political sense eclipsed Sumner's, and with this recognition, they became friends. Sumner was among the first to see Lincoln as great. Lincoln was often annoyed and frustrated by Sumner (he tended to have that effect on everyone but Longfellow), but came to see something invaluable in him— absolute moral courage.

The people of his state had seen this quality when Sumner was a young man who took on the Roberts case in 1845, standing as plaintiff's cocounsel with Robert Morris, a black lawyer. They lost the case, but they made a legal argument that would lead a century later to *Brown v. Board of Education*, which called for the end of school segregation in America. It was in this period that the young lawyer was adrift, unsure about the law as a profession, and his friendship with Longfellow was a steadying influence, one he would rely on the rest of his life. Certainly, when Sumner was caned by a Southern congressman on the floor of the Senate in 1856, and forced into semiretirement for three years to recover from his wounds, Fanny and Henry were the ones there to help in his recovery and subsequent return to the Senate.

Longfellow shared Sumner's strong abolitionist views, but except for publishing some antislavery poems in 1842, Longfellow abhorred public speaking and controversy. In fact, Sumner had written Longfellow in Europe the year before, asking him to address slavery in his poetry: "Oh! I long for those verses on slavery. Write some stirring words that shall move the whole land."

It was almost as if the two close friends were complementary—one political and public, in contrast with the other, who was poetic and private. Sumner, like his friend, has suffered in the fame game, becoming somewhat lost in our history's pages, and occasionally derided by some historians as emotionally frantic, fraught, and extremist. While Longfellow may never become popular again, it is becoming clear that Sumner's reputation is at last recovering, his courage and farsighted qualities becoming apparent. He took a great hit with a severely critical two-volume biography by David Herbert Donald that essentially portrayed his abolitionism as just short of a symptom of neurosis. Donald's resolute lack of sympathy for Sumner is at last being reexamined, and historians are placing Sumner back into the discussion of our greatest senators and essential political visionaries.

Many long decades of "lost cause" historians, convinced that the Civil War was "an unnecessary war," and that Reconstruction had been a mistake, tended to misidentify abolitionism, not the existence of slavery itself, as the true cause of the war. After the civil rights era, historians shifted from these old approaches and became more sympathetic to Sumner's radicalism. Yes, he had been a troublemaker and a continual thorn in the side of the senate, but perhaps the people who flocked to join his miles-long funeral cortège knew him better than those who had dismissed him for so long.

Longfellow, who had buried so many loved ones, now

joined the throng in 1874 to say farewell to his closest friend.
As a pallbearer, he was astonished that "he heard the first
bluebirds singing." He later wrote a poem about Sumner that,
with Longfellow's usual emotional reticence, does not mention his friend's name—except by inference, using the setting
of Mount Auburn to devastating effect. Evoking the way the
Charles River wraps around the cemetery, Longfellow alludes
to the senator's first name:

> River, that stealest with such silent pace
> Around the City of the Dead, where lies
> A friend who bore thy name, and whom these eyes
> Shall see no more in his accustomed place

And then, almost in answer to critics who claim Longfellow never took a chance in his poetry, he compares the rising
mists off the river to the dew that settles on a corpse: "And
gray mists arise / Like damps that gather on a dead man's
face."

Longfellow would join his friend at Mount Auburn in
1882, and his children each in turn. I believe he would have
well understood his fellow poet Robert Creeley's hope that it
was a good destiny to "one / way or other to / come, go with
them."

"So Young and Victorious"

On a golden late September afternoon in 2012, a small crowd gathered to dedicate one of Mount Auburn's most pressing preservation projects. We were celebrating the completion of two years of repairs to the Robert Gould Shaw monument. Its surface had been cleaned and carefully conserved, old cracks were sealed, and the family lot was set off with new plantings and a restored Victorian cast-iron fence. This spot, just to the right of Bigelow Chapel and near the massive, mysterious statue of the great Sphinx, is now perhaps the most visited place in Mount Auburn.

After the 1989 release of *Glory*, a movie about the Civil War travails of the first black soldiers in the Union army, more and more people came to visit the Shaw family lot. They were clearly moved by the film's portrayal of the twenty-five-year-old white officer who, in July 1863, led his untested troops to the lethal parapets of the seemingly impregnable Fort Wagner guarding Charleston Harbor. Along that sandy South Carolina shore, nearly half of Shaw's men died in a failed night attack—but the North could no longer doubt the fighting spirit of those black troops, nor their desire to fight for their own freedom. By the end of the war, one in ten Union soldiers would be black. This little-remembered fact was decisive in the war's outcome.

After thankful remarks from Massachusetts governor

Deval Patrick, a memorial wreath was solemnly laid before the impressive family monument. Then the evening calm was shattered with a reverberating rifle salute from members of the present-day Massachusetts 54th Volunteer Regiment Honor Guard. I wondered how many of these visitors realized that the Robert Gould Shaw listed on the large brownstone monument was in fact the young colonel's grandfather, a wealthy Brahmin businessman.

Though Colonel Robert Gould Shaw's presence at Mount Auburn is significant, his body was never returned to Boston. His parents insisted his body remain buried in Fort Wagner's sandy trenches alongside the free black men he led into battle. Many other abolitionist heroes have faded into footnotes, but the commemorative plaque on the Shaw family monument honoring the young colonel is now one of the most evocative in Mount Auburn. I thought of Robert's virtually forgotten sister, Josephine, buried nearby in the family lot of her husband, Charles Russell Lowell Jr. For me, Josephine Shaw Lowell remains as great a hero as her celebrated brother. Her long career as a social reformer began not only with the loss of her beloved brother, Rob, but also, a short year later, the loss of her husband, killed at the Battle of Cedar Creek. Somehow, in an era hardly encouraging of women's public leadership, she managed to turn her grief into a magnificent life of social service.

Josephine Shaw was known as Effie, the fourth of five children born into a family of wealthy idealists. The strong-willed child grew into a beautiful young woman. Educated in France and Italy as well as in her home country, she was remarkably bright, and she was determined to use her considerable gifts. Like the rest of her family, she believed strongly in abolitionism and supported the Northern cause for more than simply the preservation of the Union.

Above all, she loved her older brother Rob, who said of his sister, "She and I have always been together, more than any other two of the family." She fully supported him when Massachusetts governor John Andrew offered the young officer the daunting commission of leading the first black regiment into the war. Though Rob at first turned the controversial offer down, his family heritage eventually overcame his fears, and he decided that he must take up the challenge of creating a black regiment. Effie gave him her full support, more than secretly wishing that she could fight as well: "I would give anything to be one of them. I cannot express what a sense of admiration and delight fills my soul when I think of the noble fellows advancing, retreating, charging and dying."

The formation of this new regiment went surprisingly quickly, and by the close of May 1863, one of the greatest crowds in Boston's history gathered to see the resolute black soldiers parade down Beacon Street past the golden dome of the state house. Shaw and his raw recruits were shipping out to the continued Union siege of Charleston Harbor. From the balcony of the family home at 44 Beacon, Shaw's family watched him proudly as he pulled up his horse, looked up and saluted them by kissing his sword. Effie would never see him again. Robert Gould Shaw would be dead and his regiment shattered within eight weeks.

The young William James was there that thrilling day to cheer on his brother "Wilky," one of Shaw's officers. William was inwardly uneasy; like so many other privileged Boston men, he was not willing to join the Union ranks. That day he wrote, on seeing Effie and her new fiancé, Colonel Charles Russell Lowell Jr.: "I looked back and saw their faces and figures against the evening sky, and they looked so young and victorious."

Colonel Shaw admired no one in the ranks so much as his

older friend Charley Lowell, and so Shaw had been delighted when Effie fell in love with the young cavalryman. Like Shaw, Lowell had proved himself to be effective and cool under fire, and he likewise had been rewarded with the rare honor of forming a new regiment. Appointed the new colonel of the 2nd Massachusetts Cavalry, the young former businessman had come back home to Boston in order to recruit his brigade, and had unexpectedly proposed to Effie Shaw in the bargain. Strong attraction, and the exigencies of war, moved things along; family lore had it that the couple met only nine times before the engagement (though Effie long remembered having met the former Harvard valedictorian when she was fifteen).

Poet and diplomat James Russell Lowell, Charley's affectionate uncle, wrote of Effie's "force of character and good sense." This character was to be severely tested when the news arrived of Rob's death. The new colonel wrote his grieving fiancée: "Rob was very happy too at the head of the regiment where he died . . . it is a very great comfort to know that his life had such a perfect ending." They were quietly married three months later.

The next year, the 2nd Massachusetts Cavalry took part in General Grant's spring movement against Lee's armies, and Lowell quickly grew in experience and calm leadership. By late summer 1864, his troops had been thoroughly tested, the group's ranks depleted by mounting casualties. Lowell's admiring men noted that he was a lucky leader, unscratched though with already twelve horses shot from under him. In October, after receiving orders to aggressively pursue Confederate cavalry in the continuing Shenandoah Valley campaign, Lowell was clearly affected by the pressure of battle. He wrote Effie, who until now had believed he led "a charmed life," a more sober assessment: "I don't want to be shot till I've had a chance to come home. I have no idea that I shall be hit, but I want so *much* not to now that it sometimes frightens me."

On October 19, 1864, Lowell's steady hand in the midst of chaos would help turn the Battle of Cedar Creek—a near disaster for the Union cavalry—into a stunning victory. Against nearly suicidal odds (and despite having yet another horse shot from under him), Lowell convinced his men to hold a deteriorating and nearly futile battle line until the confused Union troops behind him could gather themselves. With this needed time, General Philip Sheridan formed an attack that resulted in a victory that was helpful in reelecting Lincoln the very next month.

As the tide was turning in the Union's favor, a minié ball slammed into Lowell's chest, collapsing a lung (already weakened by a prewar bout of tuberculosis). Lowell demanded to be placed back on his horse, and then was struck again, the bullet slamming from shoulder to shoulder, paralyzing him from the neck down. It would take a day for him to die. Orders already sent appointing him brigadier general came just hours too late for him to receive the news. He died just before his wedding anniversary, and weeks before his thirtieth birthday. Most haunting of all, just a month before, Effie had given birth to their child, a girl she named Carlotta. She returned to Staten Island to live with her parents and sisters, but her depression took a long time to lift, and in some ways she never recovered. She wore black the rest of her life and never remarried.

Yet Effie eventually returned to society in a forceful way; she had a more than forty-year career as a tireless philanthropist. What she had learned as a young woman in helping to form a New York soldiers' aid society would bear much fruit, starting with her determination to address what she felt had been the root cause of the war. Setting aside her grief, she found herself traveling to Richmond and Petersburg, Virginia, to help supervise instruction at new schools for formerly enslaved children. Her biographer, Joan Waugh, concludes, "After the war, Effie no longer thought of herself as an individual, free to do this and that as she pleased. She believed that the war obligated her to make the world a better place, as her brother and husband would have had they lived."

Unquestionably true, but Effie's steely intelligence and deeply religious appetite for reform were already firmly in place, and these tendencies would save her. By the time the Freedmen's Society's work drifted to conclusion in 1872, Effie was already firmly on course for her true life's work—to effectively address urban poverty in all its manifestations, especially in women's lives. She took as her model Dorothea Dix, who had in the years before the Civil War honed her skills as a publicist, a lobbyist, and a politician.

In 1876, Governor Samuel Tilden appointed her the first female commissioner of the New York State Board of Charities, and she was truly on her way, determined that well-intentioned charities get out of each other's way and become more effective agents of change. She believed the poor needed this effectiveness more than they needed sentiments, and she worked to see that they saw more of it. She fused a humane religious sensibility with a "scientific" attitude that was unsentimental and unsparing in its refusal to accept ineptitude. Effie could show irritation at "carelessness"—but she had another side, writing to a friend: "If it could only be drummed into the rich that what the poor want is fair wages and not little doles of food, we should not have this suffering and misery and vice."

But she was more than an adept political appointee—she was founder supreme of one group after another: the New York Charity Organization in 1882, the House of Refuge for Women in 1886, the Women's Municipal League in 1894, the Civil Service Reform Association in 1895, and, perhaps most importantly, in 1890, the New York Consumer's League, which tried to improve the deplorable working conditions of the city's working women. She had made such a civic impact on New York that, seven years after her death from cancer in 1905 (lamenting that she had had to wait "forty one years for Charley"), the city dedicated to her the first civic monument to a woman. The graceful and imposing pink granite fountain today is still a beloved site in Bryant Park. Charles Eliot, the president of Harvard, wrote the inscription, noting "the strong and beautiful character of Josephine Shaw Lowell / ... sincere candid courageous and tender / bringing help and hope to the fainting / and inspiring others to consecrated labors."

Sister and brother now both have their monuments. In Boston, people today still come and stand in wonder before the bronze bas-relief masterpiece by Augustus Saint-Gaudens dedicated to Shaw and his regiment. Set along the parade path of the 54th's moment of glory, the monument displays the resolute Robert Gould Shaw on horseback among his striding men, all moving toward their joint fate. William James, in his 1892 speech dedicating the Beacon Street memorial, spoke of a "lonely kind of courage (civic courage we call it in times of peace)."

In speaking of Robert, he did not openly allude to Josephine. A woman's courage was seldom saluted in that era, but no doubt there were some in that crowd remembering the young widow and what she made of a blasted world she inherited. She would receive no ten-gun salutes, no memorial wreaths. But civic courage of her kind—that survives.

The triangle of sacrifice of Rob, Charley, and Effie is remarkable, yet their shared loss also stands for so many other stories equally poignant, equally haunting. When you come to really read Mount Auburn, you begin to see and understand the slopes, dips, and undulations of the landscape—and you begin to properly read the rends and rips across the social fabric that all these hundreds of Civil War era memorials represent.

War creates loneliness and loss, but here it is the Civil War that is the fierce and unrelenting dividing line separating not only one era from another but, in hundreds of lives, creating a separation that no memorial can mend or heal. If it is hard for us moderns to truly understand the psychic toll and burden infant death represented in the historic core of the cemetery, then it is equally hard for us to enter into what Drew Gilpin Faust, president of Harvard, calls *This Republic of Suffering*, to comprehend the stunning cost these years of war represent, the young lives torn and shattered. The ties linking Mount Auburn and Harvard are evident and understandable, so when Faust went on tour to publicize her best-selling book about death and the Civil War, one of her first stops was Story Chapel, for an appearance before a full house. She movingly told the story of Henry Ingersoll Bowditch, who lost his son Nathaniel in 1863, and who recovered his body for burial at Mount Auburn. "Bowditch supplemented the formal rituals of religion with rituals of his own. . . . For Nat's grave at Mount Auburn Cemetery, Bowditch designed another embodiment of his life, exactly copying his sword in stone to serve as a monument."

The number of Civil War dead in Mount Auburn remains grim proof of the point Louis Menand made in *The Metaphysical Club*—that the old verities that fueled and comforted the young republic did not, and could not, cross over into the postwar era. The violent price America paid for the conflict was simply too steep. The brutal toll can be seen everywhere at Mount Auburn.

One of the verities that the Civil War called into question was exactly the comfort Mount Auburn was designed to provide—the idea of a death fused with beauty.

SPRING

For the past twenty years, every March 20th David Barnett takes a long and comprehensive walk over the grounds looking for signs that winter's back is broken, that spring is pushing up and out across the landscape he loves. One year, he embarked through eight inches of snow. Another year the day was sunny and eighty degrees—New England is, as he says, "variable." (Mark Twain said of our weather that if you didn't like what you had, you should just wait ten minutes.)

On this day, the leaf buds are springing forth, but the bulbs are not pushing up just yet. The snow cover is fast receding, with large plowed ridges of heavy ice-glazed snow evaporating as quickly as they are melting beneath. As the last snow patches on the lawns fade away, the open ground receives the sun hungrily, speeding the process. The brown stubbled grass, dormant but not dead, will be greening up by early April; it will have its first mowing by the middle of the month. As he goes, Barnett makes mental notes of all that the ground crews will need to repair and otherwise see to. Already, the ground staff is starting its first major job: gathering up thousands of pounds of sticks and broken limbs.

Witch hazel is the first signal of change, emerging in late February if snow lets it. Barnett emphasizes that "spring is now clearly backing up"; the natural order that we have seen for so long is shifting rapidly as we look on helplessly.

Because of climate change, Barnett and his staff tabulate spring's return not only to lift their morale; they are tracking a transformation that is frightening to contemplate.

Usually by the time of Barnett's March walk there is a carpet of blue emerging under beech trees, the small blue scilla bulbs showing at last. All four major species of maple—Norway, sugar, red, and Japanese—force their leaf buds along each stem and branch, and then the oaks, and the dogwoods. "This is the time to look more closely," says Barnett. "Something exciting is going on. We do something more powerful here than simply preserving a historic landscape. What we do here is work with nature to inspire, to offer a space of meditation, a connection with the world. It is hard to ignore that we are seeing something so powerful each year that you can only call it spiritual."

The grounds crew closely surveys what has not made it through the rough months of winter, and pays close attention to all that is coming to life, all that is flowering. By early May, everything is blooming riot, and the staff is racing to catch up with all that is in transformation. The dozens of large flower beds and the carefully pruned flowering shrubs that wind along and behind monuments now reveal why all the months of preparation and protection mattered, as their fruit, seed, and petals swell and expand. Azalea bushes bloom in whites, pinks, and reds everywhere, and the rhododendrons and viburnums begin to flower as well. Beds of flowers erupt in bright profusion and the buds on the trees uncurl their leaves. Now the blooms of magnolias, the most primitive of all flowering plants, join in, showy in April and still magnificent into May, when the skies fill with birds.

Often, the first sign is the "kong-er-ee" of the red-winged blackbird, harbinger of songs to come, then the eastern phoebe—early birds. The suddenly blazing park is full of dozens of warbler species, as the birds descend to feed and mate, which in turn draws in hundreds of birders (much more on them later) each May Day. Red-tailed hawks keenly survey their territory and wheel the sky, waiting. Most strangely, to me, is the first sighting of strutting lines of wild turkeys cutting through the cemetery, with their resemblance not to the placid, plump farm-bred turkeys raised for your Thanksgiving, but to Spielberg's *Jurassic Park* dinosaurs. They are lean, mean pecking machines. A warning: some years, they can get a little aggressive by the time of summer heat. They have been known to nip at walkers— so pay them respect.

In early morning, and at dusk, Mount Auburn is a well-populated place of wildlife, with skunks, possums, coyotes, and red foxes coming up from hidden places along the Charles River and moving into the thickest pockets of trees and shrubs. Staff fiercely protect the ingeniously tucked-away dens of young fox pups (kits, to be precise) that dot the grounds. Squirrels, chipmunks, and raccoons race and dart about the place, in quickened assertion of their right to live, to feed, to bear their young. They move quickly, instinctively aware that spring in New England is less a season than the briefest of moments, a frenzy of transition from the stasis of winter to the shimmering heats of summer.

Going Over the Ground

Bigelow Chapel was chilly and empty, with only a small family gathering in the wooden pews below me. I had been asked two days before to lead a service for an elderly woman I did not know, and though I was extremely busy, I said yes, I could be there.

It is always hard to be invited into an unknown family's grief—too many complicated feelings, agendas, disappointments, incoherent rawness to sense your way into. A sister and a brother, each surrounded by their immediate families, sat across from each other so that, as I spoke, I looked back and forth between them, from left aisle to right, absorbing what I could from these strangers' faces, noting how they held their grief in the late morning light.

Soon we were bundled into black cars to wind our way to a far corner of the cemetery. As we slowly dipped and rose along the wintry avenues, I quickly lost all sense of where we were heading. At last, the silent bustle of funeral attendants and their black cars signaled we were there. The black of an open grave was a gap against the crust of grainy snow. I have long forgotten the words I said graveside, but strangely I have not forgotten the sharp snap of sticks and the caw of hovering blackbirds as I finished and stepped back.

The son thanked me as we walked back to our cars, adding, "I liked what you said about coming back here again through the years . . . couldn't help but think of Rupert Brooke's words, 'We must go over the ground again.' "

The next week, he wrote me, again thanking me for capturing something of the essence of his mother, and then added, "I was only part right about the 'going over the ground again' citation." It was Edmund Blunden, not Brooke. Blunden, who survived the lethal insanity of Ypres and the Somme, wrote about his war experiences virtually every day until his death in 1966, in calmly understated poetry and memoirs. The son added, " 'Going over the ground again' is so very evocative and comprehensive—on many levels. We were so very fortunate to have come across your path for those brief hours."

While I may never find that particular spot again, others will, and memory will have its sway. That phrase, "going over the ground," haunts me.

Mine Eyes Have
Seen the Glory

There are three songs associated with Mount Auburn and, despite their having been written well over a hundred years ago, each is instantly recognizable and beloved still.

Longfellow's Civil War poem, "I Heard the Bells on Christmas Day," prompted by despair over the wounding of his son, Charley, in battle, was ultimately an affirmation of peace. The carol's ingenious use of rhythm imitating pealing bells gives his meditation universal appeal. Another Mount Auburn "resident," Phillips Brooks—the famed nineteenth-century rector of Trinity Church in Boston, wrote a poem while on a trip to the Holy Land, and his verse was turned into an enduring, and endearing, carol—"O Little Town of Bethlehem."

But the song most identified with Mount Auburn was written by poet and women's rights activist Julia Ward Howe; we know it today as "The Battle Hymn of the Republic." She heard the melody sung by soldiers to an existing song, "John Brown's Body," during a November 1861 visit to Washington, DC, accompanied by her husband, Samuel Gridley Howe. It was early in the war and the couple, always at the forefront of reform, wanted to see what life was like in the crowded Union camps. Samuel was already a leader in the newly formed US Sanitation Committee, precursor to the American Red Cross, but Julia Ward Howe wondered: how could she make some

kind of contribu-
tion to the great
cause?

After the couple
reviewed the troops on
parade, their carriage
was delayed by the crush
of marching regiments. To
pass the time, the Massachusetts group sang songs, including
one they had just heard the soldiers singing: "John Brown's
body lies a'mouldering in the grave, His soul is marching on."
Her minister, the Reverend James Freedman Clarke, wondered if Howe could write new words to the stirring tune.

The melody remained lodged in her mind as she and her
husband went back to the Willard Hotel in the city. After
sleeping soundly, she woke in the early dawn, long lines of a
lyric swirling in her mind. She knew if she went back to sleep
she might lose the words forever, "so, with a sudden effort, I
sprang out of bed, and found in the dimness an old stump
of a pen which I remembered to have used the day before. I
scrawled the verses almost without looking at the paper." The
earlier sight of hundreds of soldiers at their firesides fueled
her passion:

> I have seen Him in the watch-fires of a hundred circling
>   camps
> They have builded Him an altar in the evening dews and
>   damps
> I can read His righteous sentence by the dim and flaring
>   lamps:
> His day is marching on.
> Glory, glory, Hallelujah!

Vivid phrases filled her mind—images of serpents, camp-fires, white lilies of Galilee, "God marching on" in the refrain. They flooded out, and soon the sheet of Sanitary Commission stationery was filled. She went back to bed. Later, her husband gone, she reviewed what she had written. Howe hastily revised and recopied the stanzas, then mailed them off to the new *Atlantic Monthly* magazine.

The song soon appeared on the magazine's cover, and Union soldiers quickly adopted it. The song was of particular interest to Chaplain Charles McCabe of the 122nd Ohio In-fantry, who sang it to fellow prisoners of war at Libby Prison in Richmond, Virginia. After release, McCabe was asked to sing "The Battle Hymn of the Republic" at a concert with President Lincoln in attendance, and the crowd was stunned by the power of the song. The audience rose and cheered, and Lincoln, tears running down his cheeks, cried out, "Sing it again!"

That emotional response was indicative of the effect of Howe's words, and through the war and in the years that fol-lowed, the song was performed in her presence hundreds of times. It fueled her fame, and by its strange, abiding appeal, gained her prominence as a social reformer—something that proved to be a problem in her marriage, though a secret de-light to her.

Howe was called, in her older years, "the queen of Amer-ica." Few progressive ventures did not reach out to her for validation. She fought for an international day of peace, to be called Mother's Day (this was to change radically after her death, becoming a more sentimental and commercial holiday); she encouraged and supported the first group of women min-isters; she worked hard for women's rights and the vote. Not everyone backed Howe's enthusiasms, but they cheered her song anyway.

Over and over, in times of crisis or duress, Americans have turned to the fierce millennial themes of the "Battle Hymn" and its apocalyptic portrayal asserting that the cause of right and freedom was firmly in the hands of a strong and powerful Divinity: "As he died to make men holy / Let us die to make men free / While God is marching on." Martin Luther King Jr. evoked the lyric both at Selma and at Memphis (in his last speech before his assassination). It was sung at the funerals of Winston Churchill, Robert Kennedy, and Ronald Reagan. After the pain and sorrow of the events of September 11, 2001, it was not surprising that the singing of the "Battle Hymn" in the National Cathedral service was both a solace and an affirmation that the suicide hijackers would not have the final word, that "He has sounded forth the trumpet that shall never call retreat."

Howe had found the words to capture America's resolute belief that the nation's unfolding embodied a cosmic plan. Her use of images from the book of Revelations is especially effective in this regard. Of course, other nations through history have believed that God was on their side—but the "Battle Hymn" did more: it conveyed that God was on the side of freedom.

Howe's was not a mild or particularly forgiving Divinity. What she saw in her vision was not only "the glory of the Coming of the Lord," but the act of "tramping out the vintage where the grapes of wrath are stored; / He hath loosed the fateful lightning of His terrible swift sword: / His truth is marching on." At the beginning of the Civil War, when it was not at all clear whether the North would win or not— or even what the ultimate purpose of the war was—Howe offered in her "Battle Hymn" ultimate clarity and surety of purpose. She was paid only four dollars for her work—but for the Union, the song was valuable beyond measure.

Julia Ward was born in New York City, the daughter of a wealthy businessman, and grew up sheltered after her mother's early death. From an early age she showed a determination to write poems, plays, and essays. When she fell in love with the much older doctor, soldier, and renowned reformer Samuel Gridley Howe and moved into Boston's rarified Beacon Hill Brahmin culture, she quickly realized that her husband was never going to encourage her ambitions. She loved her stiff and righteous husband, but it was never a smooth, or particularly fulfilling, marriage. They both loved their six children, and Julia proudly supported her husband's many pursuits, particularly his directorship of the Perkins School for the Blind, but such encouragement was not returned. She wrote of her frustration many times, often in a diary that she knew her husband would later read. In 1865, she wrote: "I have been married twenty-two years today. In the course of this time I have never known my husband to approve of any act of mine. . . . Books, poems, plays, everything has been contemptible or contra band in his eyes, because it was not his way of doing things."

Because she left such records behind and outlived her husband by decades, her renown not only came to overtake her husband's earlier fame, but in some sense began the modern dismissal of Samuel Gridley Howe as an admittedly difficult character. He had not wanted Julia to be a writer or public figure, and it is ironic that her fame now eclipses his.

After graduating from Harvard Medical School in 1824, Samuel refused the easy path to wealth and instead decided to offer his services to the embattled Greek army fighting for independence against the stronger Ottoman Empire. The recent death by fever of the poet Byron, who had also gone to the aid of the Greek cause, showed how desperately Samuel's medical skills were needed. His brave service (a result of which he suffered the effects of malaria the rest of his life) was later rewarded by Greece with the award of Chevalier, as a Knight of St. George. He returned home with Byron's helmet, the poet's fame adding to Samuel's American renown.

Returning to Boston, Samuel quickly caught the public's imagination with his dedication to education of the deaf, in particular the education of a young girl named Laura Bridgman, born deaf, blind, and mute, with no senses of taste or smell. When the internationally best-selling novelist Charles Dickens made his first visit to America, he especially asked to visit the Perkins School for the Blind. (Sadly, in my research for this book, I have been unable to establish that Dickens ever visited Mount Auburn, as has been often claimed. He did record in *American Notes* having visited "Mount Auburn," but it referred to a later renamed rural burial ground in Cincinnati, Ohio. However, Dickens does record many walks with Longfellow so, on the other hand, it seems unlikely they would not have walked the short distance to the grounds . . . Case still open.)

Dickens left a vivid account of having seen Samuel Howe work with the thirteen-year-old New Hampshire girl, Laura Bridgman. The world wondered at Bridgman's ability to spell out her thoughts into Howe's open palm, and at their ready conversations. Bridgman even asked Dickens how *Oliver Twist* would end. No one had thought such communication was possible, but Howe was a determined man—eager to prove to skeptics that the lives of the blind could be free and opened up. His partnership with Bridgman was an exploration into the possible. He later said that the girl was like a person alone and helpless in a deep, dark pit, and that he had let down a cord in the hope that she might find and seize it by chance; then, by hanging on, she would be drawn up into human connection.

Forty years later, a distraught Alabama mother would read Dickens's account of Bridgman and her teacher and write to the Perkins School for help. Could they send someone to help her little girl, who was also deaf, blind, and mute? The young girl's name was Helen Keller.

It was an era in which it seemed perceived limits were meant to be broken. Much of Howe's work—including his efforts alongside Dorothea Dix to revolutionize the care of the mentally ill, his dedication to reform of prisons and workhouses, and his support, with Horace Mann, for public education—may seem second nature to us now, but these ideas were then revolutionary and considered controversial, and they should not be overlooked. The work energized Howe, but it was his directorship of the Perkins School that made him famous and gave him the leverage to advance in other areas.

There was no stopping Howe, especially with his close circle of reform-minded friends—including Longfellow, Sumner, Horace Mann, and James Russell Lowell—gathered round him in a men's group that Julia called "the mutual admiration society." There were few reform movements that some combination of these friends did not support—in fact, Howe was out to so many meetings that Julia sang to their children, "Oh, Daddy, where have you been? / With Mann and Sumner, a-puttin' down sin."

Some early friends cooled their connections when Samuel's passion for abolitionism took possession of his soul, but he was set on his course. (In fact, it took some time for his wife to catch up with his dangerous interest, though she eventually did.) Supporting nonviolent abolitionists such as William Lloyd Garrison was, in his view, not enough. When radical John Brown came to Boston to raise funds, Samuel, Theodore Parker, and a small circle of donors formed a secret society that backed Brown financially—though it still remains unclear exactly how much, or how little, Samuel knew about Brown's Harper's Ferry plans. When the nation was shocked by Brown's failed slave uprising (and Brown's subsequent hanging), Samuel and others were in genuine danger of arrest for conspiracy, so he hastily paid a convenient visit to Canada until things quieted down.

"Chev," as he was known to many, was still a radical at heart, but by the time war came he was advanced in years and, so, gladly took leadership in the newly formed US Sanitary Commission. This was how the couple came to be in Washington at the soldiers' encampment, and how Samuel Gridley Howe's long-held worst fear—of his wife's literary ambitions reaching unlikely and stunning fruition—came to pass.

Yet as fraught as the couple's marriage was, they came with the years to a more mellow and appreciative state. When Samuel died in 1876, after writing Julia a letter addressed to "My Dear New Friend," she mourned him and remembered his heroic stature despite the flaws. She did not, however, hesitate to start leading the life she had long dreamed of—through thirty-four years of widowhood, she vowed to make as much of a difference as her energies allowed. When asked her aim in life, she replied simply, "To learn, to teach, to serve, to enjoy!"

Before the founding of Memorial Day, Union soldiers' families and veterans created Decoration Day, held in late May, to remember the dead. Julia Ward Howe, in 1901, wrote, "In the afternoon, Maud and I drove out to Mount Auburn to visit the dear graves. We took with us the best of the birthday flowers, beautiful roses and lilies. I could not have much sense of the presence of our dear ones. Indeed, they are not there, but where they are, God only knows."

This passage, in which Julia's devotion and wonderment are equal, shows how far the New England mind had traveled from its old sureties about heaven and reunion after death. The old matriarch of Boston culture would eventually join her family with her interment there in 1910, as the blind children of the Perkins School sang the "Battle Hymn" one last time.

One spring morning, my wife and I sought out the Howe family lot along Spruce Avenue and found the couple's gravestones next to one another, tucked behind that of their son Sammy, who had died in 1863. Atop Julia's monument was an array of small stones, sprigs of new leaves, and flowers left in memorial by visitors. Her husband's monument, however, was bare.

The Time of the
Singing of Birds

As people discovered I was writing about Mount Auburn, the typical response was, "Oh, I love the birds!" Over and over again—from visiting Californians, to an octogenarian living on my street, to a friend I have known for years who unexpectedly revealed a love of bird-watching at Mount Auburn—I have been deluged with this surprisingly deep attraction to birding. Now when I visit the place, I wonder what percentage of the people I pass are there just for the birds. I suspect—and so does the staff—that the birds are the prime attraction.

Mount Auburn would not cease to exist if all birds decided to swerve away in their migrating practices—or worse, simply begin to decline in numbers in an increasingly hot world—but something essential to its beauty would be drastically affected, and it most certainly would never be the same. The year-round bird residents—the crows, blue jays, sparrows, chickadees, and cardinals—would continue to faithfully populate the landscape, but much of the color and happy frenzy would be lost forever.

Within Mount Auburn's first decade, visitor Harriet Martineau noted that it was an Eden for the avian flocks as well as for the dead. "It is a mazy paradise, where every forest tree of the western continent grows; and every bird to which the climate is congenial builds its nest. The birds seem to have found out that within that enclosure they are to be unmolested; and there is a twittering in every tree. The clearings are few; the woods preside, with here and there a sunny hill-side, and a shady dell; and a gleaming pond catching the eye at intervals."

What was true then remains true now. I was surprised how often the needs of birds came into conversations with staff. The sighting of red fox cubs of course excites everyone, but the ongoing welfare of the avian residents and visitors alike was ever-present. As all living creatures do, birds seek out an environment that harbors them and supports their needs. They seek seeds, berries, easy access to water, shade to rest and hide within. (Birds of prey seek chipmunks, which the cemetery has in teeming abundance.) When waves of migrating birds fill the skies overhead in late April and early May, the curve of the Charles River and the attractive green expanse of the cemetery lure them down by the thousands, and suddenly Mount Auburn is one of the prime birding spots in America. Ornithologists call this kind of space a "migrant trap," though there is nothing dangerous about landing here. Everything has been laid out for their benefit.

And once the birds fill this garden, a similar migration of thousands of birders clutching *Sibley* guides, notebooks, and binoculars cannot be far behind. For six weeks in the spring, and to a lesser extent in the much more extended reverse migration in the fall, Mount Auburn is a circus of color and crowds—a lively chaos. As soon as I came to understand this startling rhythm of the year, I began to see Mount Auburn as a kind of birding Brigadoon. Catch the festival as you can— the swarms of bright travelers won't be here for long.

But as I got to talk to people who love Mount Auburn all year long, I began to see something else about birding here that undergirds the fame of the great migration—and that is that much of the history of American ornithology is quietly embedded here, in these small acres. Birders everywhere know Mount Auburn as a prime birding spot to visit, but not all realize their passion (more than a hobby for so many) has important roots right here, in a garden poised between Cambridge and Watertown. Christopher Leahy, in his entertaining pamphlet *Birds and Birding at Mount Auburn Cemetery*, calls it a "hallowed shrine of American ornithology."

If you are a Boston bird person, you will have likely heard of the Nuttall Ornithological Club, one of America's oldest and most honored birder organizations. Formed in 1873, it was named for English naturalist Thomas Nuttall who, during his time at Harvard fifty years before, began collecting bird specimens—mostly with a gun. There was, of course, no digital camera to "tag" a rare species back then, so acquiring stuffed creatures was the way it was done. By the time Nuttall returned to England in 1842, a community of bird-watchers had begun to form in the Cambridge area.

Among notable members of the group was a man raised less than a mile from Mount Auburn, William Brewster, who had grown up in its vales and forests. When Brewster died and was buried at Mount Auburn in 1919, he had become one of America's greatest birders. Not only did he form the Nuttall Club at Harvard, but as founder and president he saw it give rise to the American Ornithologists' Union. He also was the first president of the Massachusetts Audubon Society. Brewster is remembered today for his concern and sorrow over the deforestation of local land and the increasing constraints on birds and other wildlife. He observed in a pained manner that "indeed, the entire region, once so secluded and attractive, has become irretrievably mutilated and hopelessly vulgarized." He worked effectively to begin the process of reforestation and the creation of better bird environments.

Anyone who loves watching birds today owes a great debt to Brewster.

Another local figure who changed ornithology forever was Ludlow Griscom, whom Leahy calls "the patron saint of American bird-watching." Griscom, who in 1959 was buried at his beloved Mount Auburn, in many ways turned birding from a scientific "hunting" pursuit into a sporting one that fused search with pleasure and wonder. As a professor of ornithology at Harvard, Griscom was frequently found at Mount Auburn, and his creation of life lists and local bird counts changed how people viewed—and worked to conserve—birds forever.

When I was young, for a time I fancied myself a budding Audubon, drawing and painting birds obsessively. But the real saga of American ornithology completely passed me by, and among the pleasures in writing *The Lively Place* was not only falling in love with birds again, but acquainting myself with dedicated souls such as Brewster and Griscom, birders who fused scientific curiosity with a passionate ecological interest. For make no mistake, birds provide a clear signal as to the overall health of our environment. Too many of the birds that John James Audubon killed, mounted, and painted in early America are gone now or endangered. The birders who crowd Mount Auburn are not just adding a rare warbler to their life lists, they are following in the long line of searchers who have dramatically increased our sensitivity to the survival prospects of earth's creatures.

In that line is the legendary Bob Stymeist, "Mayor of Mount Auburn," a committed birder since the age of twelve whose more than fifty years of leading groups at Mount Auburn, assisting and mentoring young birders, and spearheading advocacy for wildlife in Massachusetts has made him a national figure in birding. *Sweet Auburn* magazine notes that he has seen over three thousand species of birds worldwide—nearly five hundred in Massachusetts and over two hundred in Mount Auburn alone—close to a record of all birds ever recorded here.

Stymeist offers this advice to new birders in the garden:

> The Dell is one of the premier spots for spring migration. I have seen, on several occasions, the ridges of the Dell with birders all around watching birds bathe in the pool or warblers darting from bush to bush. The area around the Auburn Lake is also a great spot where one can often see a Water Thrush or a Swamp Sparrow feeding along the edge. Halcyon Lake and Willow Pond are also good spots.

This is good advice from the man who knows.

Standing with David Barnett early one morning at the top of the cross walks running steeply above Consecration Dell, I can see just what Stymeist is advising. From this height, you can look out and gaze directly into the tops of the huge trees; you are able to see into the birds' "living rooms." They are not high above you shrouded in limbs, but right on your level. It is exhilarating, and it is no wonder that many months of the year as many as a hundred birders can be found ranged around the crown of the dell.

To see a pair of bright-orange-and-black Baltimore orioles (as many as twelve "partners" have been seen at Mount Auburn in a spring season) weaving their unique bowl-shaped nest is to experience something you never forget. To meet the stoic stare of a great horned owl from his hollowed-out nest in a seventy-foot-high tree is worth as many treks as you have to take to see it. To be reading a worn epitaph and look up and see a red-tailed hawk surveying his territory from a funereal urn is to really know Mount Auburn. In truth, the birds rule the place.

Having met many dedicated scientific bird watchers, I need to confess that I am unlikely ever properly to follow in their footsteps. I have my own bird bible to follow, the English best seller *How to Be a (Bad) Birdwatcher*. Author Simon Barnes makes a distinction between watching for birds and enjoying birds for the sake of wonder. Obviously, this is a bit of a rhetorical point, but Barnes believes more people would follow birds if they were assured that they didn't have to count them or track them down like missing prey—just glory in them. He says he does not go bird-watching: "I am birdwatching. Birdwatching is a state of being, not an activity. It doesn't depend on place, on equipment, on specific purpose, like, say fishing. . . . It is a matter of keeping the eyes and ears and mind open. It is not a matter of obsession, not at all. It is just quiet enjoyment." He maintains birds are the most direct route to experiencing glory in life, and I can't argue with him. Barnes treasures the preservation of special places for birds, but cautions that any place is good for bird-watching. "Each one is jolly nice on its own, but it is the totality of these places that counts. They are ordinary and they are many, and, without them, there would be no birds and no life worth living for humans, either."

On this basis, I am proud to be a bad bird-watcher.

So the renewal of my love affair with birds continues, a happy by-product of this literary endeavor, but with one strange frustration: I have looked often, but I just can't seem to spot a great blue heron at Mount Auburn, and it's killing me. Most everyone at Mount Auburn has seen one, as the heron loves to delicately step along the shallow edges of Willow Pond and Auburn Lake, ready to spear a flicker of fish. They are hardly rare. But for some reason, the great blue seems just beyond my sight.

I suppose everyone has experienced something similar— one item on a life list that stubbornly won't appear (probably a part of what compels the collecting spirit in the first place). Peter Matthiessen, in his classic travel book *The Snow Leopard*, records his effort to set eyes on one of the rarest animals on earth, one hardly ever seen by humans—the reclusive snow leopard of Nepal. In the end, Matthiessen's Buddhist beliefs are strengthened by the realization that the value of the snow leopard lies in its *not* being seen—that the seeking of that sleek animal was simply one path to knowing the truth of our being.

The thousands of birders who crowd Mount Auburn each year are an essential part of its allure. They are fellow searchers of something just beyond their ken, attracted by that glimpse of something flashingly alive. As participants in the hope of spring's renewal, they are joined, perhaps unknowingly, to the ancient biblical words inscribed on William Brewster's Quincy granite gravestone:

> For, lo, the winter is past,
> The flowers appear on the earth;
> The time of the singing of birds is come.

"My Story Ends
in Freedom . . ."

T here is an ancient Roman saying: "Death renders all
equal."

It is a temptation to think of Mount Auburn solely as the
final repository of the famous and the educated, America's
elite. Yet one of the most distinctive things about the place is
that it was, from its founding, explicitly open to any and all,
in demonstration of death as the ultimate democracy.

We have so often chosen to segregate ourselves in death
as we do in life. When the Reverend Martin Luther King Jr.
said that the most segregated hour in American life was eleven
o'clock on Sunday morning, he might just have well added the
hour of our death to his accounting. Yet Bigelow's visionaries were never bound by such cultural and soul-constricting
strictures. From the very first, Mount Auburn was open to all
regardless of religion, race, class, or status. One of the most
quietly effective gravestones here is that of a tailor named Peter Byus, of whom virtually nothing is known other than that
he was born in Virginia a slave and, at the age of thirty-six,
"he fled to Boston for Freedom where he resided for the last
thirty years. He died the 27 of February 1867. Aged 66 years."
His friends bought this gravestone, which features a carving
of a kneeling man raising his arms in thanks or salutations,
broken shackles at his feet. They planted a dogwood over
his grave.

The model for Longfellow's poem "The Village Black-smith"—the burly workman Dexter Platt—is buried here, so too is the owner of Platt's home after his death, the escaped former slave Mary Walker. Fifty-four Brattle Street—now the site of the busy Cambridge Center for Adult Education—is the former home of a mother forced to live out one of the hardest quandaries of freedom imaginable. Walker's own emancipation for many years came at the cost of having to be separated from the children and mother she loved.

She is just one of the many African American figures whose stories are being recovered by Mount Auburn staff and by historians and families searching for forgotten roots. In 2012, Duke historian Sydney Nathans published *To Free a Family: The Journey of Mary Walker*, a startling reconstruction of Walker's nearly twenty-year struggle to reunite her family after she escaped from slavery. After reading the harrowing account, which stands for the stories of millions of lives under the shroud of enslavement, I went to pay my homage at Walker's grave at Mount Auburn.

So many beautiful monuments have affected me through the years, and even more present themselves along new walks, but if I had to choose my favorite, it would be Walker's. She is buried alongside her son Bryant. The seven-foot-tall marble obelisk reads: "Mary Walker, born in Orange County, North Carolina, died in Cambridge, November 10, 1872." Perched at the apex of the gently narrowing column is a somewhat simple winged dove—its arching neck and outstretched wings give a lovely sense of peace infused with flight yet to come. It is quite haunting. Even if you did not know her story, the monument would give you pause.

Born in 1818, in Piedmont, North Carolina, Mary Walker was a skilled seamstress who earned the longtime trust of her owners, the wealthy Cameron family. Year after year, they brought her with them to Philadelphia each summer to care for their children. When Walker learned that she would be sold (and separated from her own three children) upon the family's return to North Carolina, the thirty-year-old mother made the heartbreaking decision to simply walk away one summer day in 1848, leaving her own mother and her children under the "ownership" of the Camerons.

The kindness and support Walker received from sympathetic employers did not ease her desperate situation or console her in her despair over her family. Against all the abolitionist ideals she believed in, she offered to pay money for the children's release. When this did not work, several abolitionist leaders, including Frederick Douglass, tried other strategies to somehow shake free her family. Nothing worked, and finally a friend wrote to the Camerons in 1859: "Her heart is slowly breaking. She thinks of nothing but her children, and speaks of nothing else when she speaks of herself at all, which is very seldom. Her mother-heart yearns unspeakably after them."

In the chaos following the outbreak of war, Mary Walker hoped something might change for her separated kin, that some new path or stratagem would finally work after so many disappointments. She even managed to gain a position working on behalf of newly freed slaves in the Sea Islands of Georgia, just to be nearer to her children. But it was only at the very close of the war, with the South collapsing and Sherman's march to the sea nearing its end, that slave owners in Raleigh, including the Camerons, surrendered and offered up their enslaved servants to Union lines.

Walker had done such a good job enlisting so many to her cause that a Union officer quickly went to the Cameron plantation in hopes of finding her children. There, he happily discovered Agnes and Bryant in good health and ready to go north (their older brother, Frank, had escaped in 1852). Within three months, both had made their way to Cambridge, where they were at last reunited with their mother who was, understandably, "wild with joy."

A happy ending . . . though life is never quite that simple, nor should the relief of one family's agony somehow mitigate what all those mothers who never found their children again were forced to endure. As you stand at Walker's family's monument today, recalling her determination to reunite her family helps us remember the vast price so many generations paid for something so simple: to be together, in life and in death.

In easy eyesight of Walker's dove monument is the grave of her friend, a woman whose bold memoir of slavery remains one of the touchstones of black women's experience. Harriet Jacobs was an important abolitionist activist and writer for decades after her escape from slavery. Jacobs's book *Incidents in the Life of a Slave Girl* is now recognized as a classic, but when she died in 1897 she was almost forgotten.

Until recently her memoir, when remembered at all, was often viewed either as having been written by her friend and editor Lydia Maria Child or as fiction. It was neither. The historian Jean Fagan Yellin did brilliant detective work in firmly establishing what should have been long apparent—that this incendiary depiction of slavery's harshest effects on women bears the stamp of a real woman's voice. Yellin took the white abolitionist writer Child at her word that she had not written this account, and painstakingly searched to find the forgotten author, Harriet Jacobs—a woman who not only saw her story of sexual abuse in slavery into print ("Slavery is terrible for men, but it is far more terrible for women.") but had the courage to return south even before the war ended to set up behind Union lines a refugee center and a school.

The work of establishing the truth about *Incidents* was a winding trail of investigation by Yellin. In truth, no one had bothered to really examine the evidence before. Yellin's work not only brought to light the truth of the memoir, but it also unveiled hundreds of important papers and letters from the entire Jacobs family, which are now being published for the first time, giving us a fuller picture of the world of black and white abolitionists that she knew so well. Jacobs, writing under the name Linda Brent when her book was published in 1861, had written a heart-rending story that cut deep because it was true. It is still difficult to read in its painful particulars. Women of the time, black or white, were not allowed to speak of loved children whose father was not their husband, or of what it took for a woman to survive sexual abuse and shame under slavery. It may have taken so long to accept this classic of American experience as true because Jacobs was far ahead of her time. Her raw and unfiltered "novel" was perhaps too violent and direct for Victorian tastes, but her grave today is becoming a place of pilgrimage.

Though Jacobs was born into slavery in Edenton, North Carolina, her early memories were largely warm and positive. Her luck continued when she was taught to read and write by an owner (such instruction was a crime throughout much of the South in that era). Things darkened when a new owner threatened the young woman with dire consequences if she did not sleep with him. Jacobs instead chose a local white lawyer to be the father of two children, a desperate stratagem that worked to hold off her owner's advances. But her defiance could last only so long. Learning that she was to be sold and separated from her children, she escaped—but into a surprising and dangerous choice of hiding.

If she had run far she would have been harshly punished when found; instead she had the wily courage to stay close, to continue to watch over her children as she was hidden away in a narrow roof space over her grandmother's house. Though she lay mostly in darkness, unprotected from heat or cold in a space where she could not completely stand up, she considered herself lucky to be able to see her children, through a bored-out spy hole, as they came and went—yet she could not call out to them, or have them come to her. She passed the endless days reading and sewing. Jacobs barely endured each winter's cold, but somehow managed—through severe illnesses and chronic stiffness, and the ongoing fear of being found—to endure this confinement for an unbelievable seven years.

Finally, when she was on the verge of being discovered, she was spirited away to the north in 1842. She joined her brother John, who was already involved in the abolitionist movement. Her children, Louisa and Joseph, had arrived before her, so her freedom meant she was reunited with them at last. With her evident intrepid spirit, Harriet quickly became an accepted activist and writer determined to add her unique story to the growing list of abolitionist accounts detailing the realities of slavery. It took her four years to get her account published, after many setbacks, and suggestions that being honest about her life was problematic (an unease she herself shared).

In her later years in Cambridge, Jacobs ran a boarding house at 127 Mount Auburn Street. There she became friends with neighbor Mary Walker. One can only imagine the stories they might have shared. After Walker's death and interment at Mount Auburn (where, in the same year, Jacobs's brother John had been buried as well), Jacobs's daughter Louisa brought her mother to Washington, DC, to live. When her mother died in 1897, Louisa chose to bring her back to Cambridge to be near her brother and old friends, offering this as the remarkable woman's epitaph: "Patient in tribulation, fervent in spirit in serving the Lord."

In these recovered stories, not only are remarkable and re-sourceful characters revealed, but entirely new angles on American history are unveiled. Just when you think that one small cemetery cannot possibly contain any more facets of our national story, enterprising historians come along to recover people like Mary Walker and Harriet Jacobs, and the revelations continue.

When my son Paul and I decided to trace the long legal saga of the 1845 *Roberts* case, from a Boston courtroom all the way to *Brown v. Board of Education* more than a century later, we realized we were shining a light into an obscure, nearly lost corner of our history. We wondered—who would care about a free black printer who sued the city of Boston to allow his daughter Sarah to attend Boston's white schools? Would anyone care how that case reverberated through history to the very steps of the Supreme Court?

But there is something joyous in finding such stories, and when you stand in front of Benjamin Roberts's gravestone today, you sense how important Mount Auburn's open spirit really is to our history. Roberts, that determined father, is just one of ninety-eight thousand souls buried here, but despite this printer's difficult and obscure life, his legal suit on behalf of his daughter changed our history, moving us from "separate but equal" to "equal rights before the law." Finding his grave here was thrilling, as we desperately searched for facts in a story where little remained of a free black community's letters and diaries, and even basic newspaper accounts. (We are still looking for the resting place of daughter Sarah.) We had to scratch for every piece of this story. But Benjamin Roberts's grave is real and solid, a place to return to. Also buried here is one of his two lawyers in the case, Senator Charles Sumner, and the judge who heard the case, Lemuel Shaw. Mount Auburn is a historical treasure trove, and I suspect we presently know only the half of it.

It is a sad truth that not all lives end fulfilled or noble. But here in these recovered stories we are reminded, however tired or cynical we grow, that some souls somehow absorb the pain and the losses, and find a little glory. Looking back at his people's struggles, before his death in 1881, the aging Roberts wrote of the "deepest and most profound astonishment of our people . . . but amid all this, we have important duties to perform. We must be true to each other. We must encourage each other."

As Harriet Jacobs said at the end of her controversial memoir: "Reader, my story ends with freedom." I have recounted the stories of a few individuals who struggled and sacrificed for their freedom and for their families', but this emancipation of course moves beyond those singular lives. The broken shackles carved on Peter Byus's marble monument are symbols of liberation for all.

Grave Words

As a minister and a voracious reader, I have seen thousands of epitaphs along the way. My favorite is mentioned in John Berendt's *Midnight in the Garden of Good and Evil*. Writing about a Savannah cemetery, Berendt notes the resting place for poet, critic, and novelist Conrad Aiken, whose sentiments were direct on one side of his monument—"Give my love to the world"—and on the other, quite grand—"Cosmic Mariner: Destination Unknown."

Writing an epitaph is an art, and a mostly forgotten one. A couple of years ago there was a *New Yorker* cartoon of a gravestone with the ornately carved word, "Whatever."

Increasingly unsure about the nature, or even the reality, of an afterlife, we grow coy, tongue-tied in fashioning last words. What is evocative and moving in one generation may well feel cloying and clichéd in the next—but that hardly matters. Here, as one walks through the grounds reading epitaphs (as best one can, with acid rain eroding all sentiments), primal emotion shines through the olden rhetoric. The hopes for reunion and eternal life are still poignant, particularly with regard to the gravestones of children, even though we may feel quite distant and disconnected from the writer's understanding of death.

For me, as well as many others, it is clear which epitaph in Mount Auburn is the most effective and beautiful. In writing a terse message to be carved in stone for future generations, it helps to be a poet comfortable in the small scale; David McCord, who wrote many books of poetry for children, was terrific in this regard. When you stand before his gravestone today, you might be caught by the way, in such small confines, it captures the long expanse of life:

> Blessed Lord, what it is to be young;
> To be of, to be for, be among—
> Be enchanted, enthralled,
> Be the caller, the called,
> The singer, the song, and the sung.
>
> Blessed Lord, what it is to be old;
> Be the teller, and not the told,
> Be serene in the wake,
> Of a triumph, mistake,
> Of life's rainbows with no pots of gold.

It is not terribly surprising that McCord chose to be buried here, as he loved all aspects of Boston and for decades edited the *Harvard Alumni Bulletin*. His graceful writing lured generations into generous college giving—"fishing," he said, "without a worm." I discovered McCord when a wise elderly member of my church gave me a laminated copy of "Youth" and "Old Age," having carried them over the years in her wallet. Like her, I have found in McCord's words a wisdom fused with rueful wit and acceptance of life's "rainbows with no pots of gold." No wonder, though McCord's poetry is seldom anthologized today, people come and stand before his grave.

Cemeteries are places of beauty, true, but they are also places of a strange, almost thrilling, realism. Some religious sensibilities have long maintained that death is itself an illusion, a mistaken apprehension. Just as the eighteenth-century philosopher George Berkeley maintained that the world was an edifice of conscious sensations and nothing more, the more empirical Samuel Johnson replied by kicking a stone, hard, and stating, "I refute thee, thus!" Like Johnson's stern kick, a walk through Mount Auburn is a lovely but quite persuasive refutation of the idea that death is not real.

SUMMER

In June, spring is generally still holding on, barely, but summer announces itself with the mountain laurel bushes popping in all their varieties, with markings of reddest pinks and whites; they are among the most spectacular of the native woodland plants. Also in early summer, Mount Auburn's roses come out, mostly climbing roses wrapped around street posts and taller grave markers. Smaller shrub rose flowers line the avenues. The roses are not generally the spectacular prize-winning sort, with top-heavy lush blooms set in ornate flower beds. These blend into the grounds, adding a gentle luster to the summer scene.

Then the heat settles in, and the mowers' rotary machinery mulches the lawn in place until September, when the grasses, depending on the rain, are almost dormant. The need to ever fertilize is now a thing of the past. The organic mulch settles into the earth, stimulating growth later on. The new lawn strategy is effective, labor-saving, and compost-friendly. The grounds are healthier, the wildlife safer, and back-breaking labor is reduced by half. Perhaps most importantly, the runoff of fertilizer into the ponds, and down into the Charles River, is eliminated.

One late July evening, David Barnett led a horticultural tour for a small group to see what was still flowering in the heat. His delight at finding the late blooms of the season was palpable, and it was hard not to get enthused when he lifted up a branch to show the white, delicate blossoms of hydrangeas, which would be flowering until the first hard frost. The summer is a quiet time for both birds and bush, but Barnett showed us that Nature in fact never relents— it keeps sending forth shoots and stems—and color, though now more subtle and harder to spy, is still everywhere.

We looked at the still waters of Willow Pond, and he showed us where a convocation of engineers and environmentalists had met the week before in an effort to make the pond friendlier to birds (particularly the blue heron, which likes to stand at the shallow end and spear a small fish or two in the dusk) and to keep the waters fresher and less stagnant for fish, water plants, and all the amphibians they want to attract to this area of the cemetery.

Barnett never seems to stop thinking about how to improve all aspects of the "conversation with Nature." Witness the new butterfly garden along the edge of the pond. Sure enough, some butterflies floated around us, but what I noticed that warm night was an equally satisfying number of "plops" of frogs and toads leaping into the pond for the night. This was satisfying progress.

After another half hour of walking, we paused to gaze at the long expanse of Auburn Lake from the south side of the grounds. Barnett shared his quiet satisfaction at how much had been achieved in his twenty years as head of horticulture, and how he had worked with Bill Clendaniel and others to implement a radical renovation of what is one of the most lovely sights here.

In the old Victorian days, Auburn Lake, like so many other places here, had been rimmed by concrete in a formal design. Though that was taken out long ago, the lake, if not dying, was starting to choke on decades of accumulated thick organic muck; sometimes in the summer heat, the lake dried up to exposed mud flats.

It was time to dredge out the old sediment and refresh the lake, which opened up an opportunity to create at the far ends a shallow shelf area better for some plants and birds ("marshy," now in a good way), and in turn deepen the center of both lake areas for clearer, healthier water. New overhanging shrubs and canopy trees were replanted all around the lake, and the end result was a splendid—and far more healthy—lake. It was a huge project, as removal of the muck required draining each basin of the lake and storing tons of rank sediment near the greenhouse for later good use on the grounds.

As he talked of all the transformations in view, Barnett said, "All that work, and now everything has settled in and looks just the way it should. It takes many years to have one's landscape work get to where you envisioned long before. It's hard to do—to see so many years ahead, and how things are to grow in place and become something wonderful like this."

I asked if it was an odd feeling to be a designer of landscapes, knowing that as the years went by one's efforts were successful only if in fact no one could possibly see your hard work; everything had to look natural, easeful—untouched, really, by human hand or thought.

He laughed. "I've never thought of that, but that's the way it is supposed to work. I wouldn't want anyone to see what we did here. They're supposed to just accept it as a place of beauty, the way it was supposed to be."

I offered him an English story I have used many times in my work, in which a parson strolls by a parishioner toiling away in his garden plot. The minister stops and offers words he thinks will be encouraging: "You and the Lord are doing fine work here in this garden."

The old man rises from his weeding, wipes his sweating brow, and mutters, "You should have seen the place when the Lord had it to himself."

"A time when the mad riot of color is behind us," is how horticultural curator Dennis Collins describes the summer. "Because there are far fewer flowers, I can see better what needs to be done all across the grounds. And we do everything we can do to make whatever blooms last longer, to keep the grounds inspiring."

The strenuous heat comes in, stressing the grounds and the wildlife, but quiet growth continues. Christopher Leahy recommends that you simply position yourself on the edge of Auburn Lake and wait: "You may be able to watch a female Baltimore oriole weave her remarkable pendulous sack nest. Or perhaps the fox family that dens in the cemetery will come down for a drink. Just watching the five distinctive species of dragonflies that inhabit this pond is a fine way to spend part of a summer's morning."

Greening

A Natural Shift

We live increasingly in an age when people no longer feel the need to maintain strong denominational ties, but we are not so far away from ancestral and lingering connections to religion's old pull. So, in the face of death, families come to Mount Auburn and decide that, after all, they need more than a quiet graveside moment for their loved ones. Seeing Story Chapel's austere beauty, or Bigelow's old Gothic power, they turn and say, unexpectedly, "We need a service." Then Tom Johnson, family services coordinator, picks up the phone and reaches out to one of his "team": a pastor, priest, rabbi, imam—some cleric he has come to trust who doesn't mind dropping his or her usual duties to serve strangers in grief. I have come to instantly recognize his voice, and the question.

In 2012, one such sorrowing unaffiliated soul sat with me, an intense musician planning a service for his young wife. She had fought off cancer for six years but had finally succumbed, leaving him and her sons bereft. Still, he wanted a service that would be more than a litany of old hymns and hollow words. He wanted beauty and poetry, and the opportunity to present a song he had written for her. Then he really surprised me. His wife had loved stand-up comedy, and since she had worked so hard at it despite her illness (and maybe because of it), she was determined that on the day of her funeral she would have the last word.

No doubt it would be the first time that Bigelow Chapel hosted a memorial service ending with video of a comic routine, the deceased's last take on life and death and the strange absurdity of it all, dying when she had so much to live for. Only her husband knew she had taped it, for this eventuality.

I said, "Well, she's a brave soul to surprise all of us like that." Her husband leaned back, relieved that I was game, that her wish would be fulfilled.

As it happened, once the shock of the screen rolling down at the close of the service had eased—her tired but determined image waving to us all, her sons gaping in stunned but delighted surprise—she did indeed make us laugh, and the tears flowed. She said goodbye as she wanted to, brave and audacious.

After the service, as family and friends lingered by her grave, I walked over to stand with Tom, to give the mourners time and privacy. It was a late spring day, with intimations of summer heat in the breeze wafting the high limbs of trees along Willow Pond Knoll. Idly, I asked Tom a question I had been pondering for a while: "How much longer do you think Mount Auburn will be able to bury people?"

He paused, considering. "Oh, I think about two hundred more years."

In April 2014, one of the most important shifts in the history of Mount Auburn took place, and it represented a huge change in our common life and our attitudes toward death.

Although it would be hard to find a more classically representative "old school" burial ground, Mount Auburn was the first spot in Massachusetts to be granted official designation as a "hybrid burial ground" by the Green Burial Council. What this means is something quite practical—families now have options beyond burying their loved ones in lined caskets or in urns filled with ashes (both previously requiring concrete lining). Natural, or "green," burial is now possible at one of the oldest cemeteries in the United States, which means you can once again be buried here in a simple shroud, or a wicker casket, or even a cardboard papier-mâché box.

You, and the container, are biodegradable—and more people than ever find this fact fits comfortably in line with their beliefs.

Candace Currie, director of planning and sustainability, took me on a tour around the cemetery, showing me spots where these new burials are now taking place or where areas are being cleared for future use by families. The tour took a while, not merely because the old electric carts are, she ruefully admits, quite slow, but because the designated spots have not been segregated into a new special section. This is in line with a historic policy (which I have found to be one of the more attractive aspects of this place) by which Mount Auburn "has no site dedicated solely to natural burials, or religious affiliations, or ethnicity, or for service to country." Rather, when an old tree dies, or when an old concrete path is pulled up to be narrower and more rustic, or when the staff simply realizes a suitable space is actually available without crowding other residents, a family may go forth.

The formerly prescribed concrete linings may all be forgotten and a more natural burial can take place; these are happening now all over the grounds. Another aspect of this new way of doing things is the greater flexibility in terms of grave markers. You can choose all varieties of marker, provided the selection fits within the "style" of the section you find yourself. The marker can be a regular erect stone, or one flush with the ground, such as those currently above Willow Pond—or, radically, no stone at all. For some spots, a small memorial plaque under a tree or a flowering shrub will be preferred—but one way or the other, you and your family have vast latitude as to how your burial site will be handled.

The staff promises that you will never be lost (GPS coordinates will be, they say, perpetual). In addition, reflecting back to Bill Bryson's horrible descriptions of the old ways, "remains will not be removed to allow for the interment of another." Some other green burial spots around the United States do not make this promise, with the thinking that when you really return to the earth, the earth can always receive more.

Bree Harvey, vice president of cemetery and visitor services, reminds us that none of this is at all out of line with Bigelow's thinking. In fact, once you read in the little red book his essay on ancient burial customs, it is surprising that it took so long to return to this freedom. Harvey writes, "More than 180 years ago, they embraced the idea that 'the elements which have once moved and circulated in living frames do not become extinct or useless after death: they offer themselves as the materials from which other living frames are to be constructed.'" Bigelow, ahead in so many aspects of culture, was certainly a radical in this. The current staff is guided by Bigelow's insight that "it is all about decomposition."

I guess it was. The following is a verse of the hymn, written by Unitarian minister John Pierpont, sung at the consecration ceremony:

> Decay! Decay! 'tis stamped on all!
> All bloom, in flower and flesh, shall fade.
> Ye whispering trees, when we shall fall,
> Be our long sleep beneath your shade!

Well, "Amazing Grace" it isn't, but it does show our forebears were more than ready for Bigelow's message.

Candace Currie is clearly excited that the place is going hybrid and that the founders are, in a way, leading them in that direction. She came to Mount Auburn twenty years ago to map trees and work on all aspects of horticultural planning and sustainability in order "to allow us to bury as long as possible," as she puts it. But now, her focus and passion has shifted dramatically, from the landscape to people's lives.

"I used to say, 'Oh, I work in horticulture,' but now what I care about is developing space for natural green burials, to help families. You can look at Mount Auburn as a marble sculpture park, but you have to learn to see deeper, to see the stories behind the stones. When someone comes to us, wanting a soft woolen shroud to cover their body and not a concrete liner and an expensive coffin, now we can respond. This is a radical movement, but it is about people." And she tells me to go back to Bigelow's ideas.

Let's face it. Normally, the subjects of decay and decomposing bodies are downers of an epic sort. But in an age where composting is getting sexy, and the green burial movement is taking off, suddenly Bigelow looks amazingly prescient. Boston was a town that loved long and challenging lyceum-style lectures, and Bigelow was a frequent, respected speaker on topics skirting the edge between science and philosophy—but the topic he chose to present to the Boston Society for the Promotion of Useful Knowledge at the Masonic Temple in 1831 was not chosen for academic reasons.

He had a specific agenda: to publicize the Mount Auburn enterprise (which had to succeed as a business, after all) and to shift public thinking on the whole topic of rural burial. On the surface, burial in a pretty landscape and not in a molder-ing slice of churchyard with bones occasionally poking out seems like an obvious choice, but custom and religious prac-tices (and, likely, professional jealousies), made the argument an urgent one.

So Bigelow faced critics, along with the curious, with a lec-ture titled "A Discourse on the Burial of the Dead." It makes interesting and persuasive reading today. After paying proper respects to the feelings of those grieved and bereaved, he hits hard, in the voice of a cool, reasoned scientist: "The progress of all organized beings is towards decay."

He proceeds from there to remind all of the "complicated textures which . . . begin to fall asunder almost as soon as life has ceased." For many pages, he reviews the ways in which we have, throughout history and largely for kings and pharaohs, tried to stave off decay, then notes the essential root fact: "In certain cases art may modify, and accident may retard, the ap-proaches of disorganization, but the exceptions thus produced are too few and imperfect, to invalidate the certainty of the general law."

And what is that general law's chief application? That this "disorganization" is a good thing, that these materials need to be unwound, untied, scattered, so that they might be em-ployed in a newly organized structure—a new body, a new plant structure. Nothing is possible without this disorganiza-tion, and everything is possible with it.

Only human beings resist this positive law. Bigelow under-stands that we prefer to think ourselves exempt from it, but we are not. We instead pour "much labor and treasure . . . to ward off, for a season, the inevitable courses of nature." He lists embalming, the placing of dust in golden urns, and the building of great edifices over old bones, "with what success, and with what use, it may not be amiss to consider." After numerous historical examples of this vain enterprise for celebrated corpses of the past, Bigelow finally lays out his cards.

"Could we, by any means, arrest the course of decay, so as to gather round us the dead of a hundred generations in a visible and tangible shape; could we fill our houses and our streets with mummies,—what possible acquisition could be more useless, what custom could be more revolting?" What indeed? Luckily for the city of Boston, and for a revolutionary new generation, a far better solution was at hand.

Without mentioning his plan, or the selling of plots, he offers a final observation: "The law of nature requires that they should molder into dust, and the sooner this change is accomplished, the better. . . . It should take place peacefully, silently, separately, in the retired valley, or the sequestered wood, where the soil continues its primitive exuberance, and the earth has not become too costly to afford to each occupant at least his length and breadth."

Few in his time, and few enough since, have been this bold, but it is impossible to understand the origin of Mount Auburn—and, by extension, understand where the green burial movement is heading—without consulting this text. These are hardly new ideas, but our general reluctance to engage with Bigelow's "general law" has made progress achingly slow. To Currie, these new practices go from allowing a family to wash and prepare a body for burial, to letting them select a willow woven casket, to permitting them to turn away from embalming fluids of all kinds. She says normal funeral home practices, such as pumping the body full of chemicals, essentially produce a slow-leaking "toxic waste dump," which eventually saturates the surrounding ground. After reading Bigelow's dismissal of efforts to delay the inevitable, I had to agree with her. To what end?

So practices all up and down the line are changing quickly,

urged on by people like Currie and author Mark Harris who, in a talk at Mount Auburn about his book *Grave Matters*, offered this long perspective: "I think we're finally seeing the wisdom of allowing Mother Nature to run her natural course." Harris hopes this movement will help us realize "that our best last act may, in fact, be the very simple one of using what remains of our physical existence to fertilize depleted soil, push up a tree, preserve a bit of wild from development, and, in the process, perpetuate the natural cycle of life that turns to support those we leave behind."

Harris's passion was fueled by a 1998 visit to the first modern natural cemetery (one that later generations may place on an equal historical footing with Mount Auburn), Ramsey Creek Preserve in South Carolina. A small thirty-acre pinewood forest, the cemetery is a place where all the elements Currie has listed for me have come together: embalming is banned and concrete vaults, as well as ornate caskets, are prohibited. "These graves," Harris adds, "weren't just part of the landscape: they were the landscape, so closely tied to the land that they were largely inconspicuous. In a hundred years, even less evidence will exist to show that a body was ever buried here. By then, these fieldstone markers will have completely weathered into the landscape, and future visitors will have to consult GPS coordinates to locate the graves of their ancestors." That was the positive; he also has been swayed by the impact of the negative—such as his estimate that a ten-acre cemetery contains enough coffin wood to build forty homes, and has enough toxic formalin to fill a backyard swimming pool. "Looked at that way, I think the local cemetery actually serves less as a bucolic resting ground for the dead than a landfill of the nonbiodegradable and hazardous materials that encase them."

But Harris believes change is possible, and shifts in burial customs could come very quickly. All we have to do is look at the rapid rise in cremation practice, here at Mount Auburn and all around the nation. In 2014, 44 percent of the country chose cremation, and it is estimated that by 2020 this will become the majority option.

During the 2012 rededication ceremony for the Shaw monument, after the parade and the speeches and the cake, everyone was milling about in a very good mood when, out of the corner of my ministerial eye, I saw, not forty feet away, a hearse pull up to the side of Bigelow Chapel. A body was wheeled in. I mentioned this to Bree Harvey, saying, "It never ceases, does it?"

"We are a functioning cemetery, and we're glad we are."

As far as we can tell, Mount Auburn built the first crematory within an existing cemetery. (Nearby Forest Hills Cemetery, in Boston, with which Mount Auburn has had a low-fever rivalry for more than a century, built its own crematory at the same time, but it is slightly outside the cemetery limits.) By the late 1880s upper class Bostonians were starting to consider cremation, so discussions began at Mount Auburn. By 1896, with the building of the new Story Chapel near the gate entrance, the old Gothic chapel near the Sphinx was available for consideration for this innovative use.

This was big news at the time. An illustration of the old chapel building in an 1899 newspaper had this caption: "The finishing touches are now being made to the finest and best equipped crematory in the world." The old interior was completely reconstructed and converted to this new function, and on April 18, 1900, the ovens—called retorts—were used for the first time. (This was only seven years after the first official cremation in Massachusetts, for the famous suffragist Lucy Stone.) In 1929 there was another renovation of Bigelow Chapel's Gothic interior and, forty years later, the old crematory was removed and new retorts built on the west side under the chapel.

Currie took me to the west basement area of Bigelow where, far out of sight of the ceremonies, receptions, and dinners above in the beautiful chapel area, the large ovens are burning, each usually for twelve hours a day. I saw the cardboard boxes where bodies lay waiting their turns, and felt the strong heat radiating from the walls. It was a stark, utilitarian set of rooms, and the Mount Auburn charm was far away. Still, Walter Morrison, a friendly, gentle man about as far from what one might expect of a person in his job, was happy to show me around. (Later, I learned that when a Mel Gibson movie was shot at the cemetery, Walter got a small role.) I got the sense that he, like Currie, thinks about the families involved—that this is personal, not a business. I liked the fact that the crematory was connected to the chapel; it made what could seem streamlined and cold (odd word in this context) almost a sacred act.

Currie and Morrison dutifully laughed when I shared an oft-used story of an elderly woman who was on her deathbed, surrounded by her anxious children. "Mom, you've never told us, do you want to be buried or cremated?"

"I don't know; surprise me."

Currie's perspective on the ecological impact of cremation was a surprise to me. I had always seen it as clean and efficient—as green as it gets. She cautioned me on my assumptions. "You are still dealing with emissions—like the mercury from the fillings of your teeth. And think of what it takes to burn a body to ashes within four hours—ovens pitched to 1,800 degrees, which takes a lot of energy. So, natural burial of bodies is still a reasonable choice."

When Clendaniel and his team embarked on the Master Plan in 1993, the question of how long they could continue to

bury—thereby fulfilling the essential purpose of the place—
was an open question. There was a growing suspicion that it
was getting as full as it could get. If that were so, then maintaining the garden/history aspect of Mount Auburn would
take over as their work. But with the rise of cremation, and
with innovative ideas from local landscape designers, all kinds
of new options suddenly arose. To their relief, all of these creative options gave the staff a sense that there was more land,
and there were more burial opportunities, than they could
ever have dreamed.

Most walkers perambulate within a quarter mile of the
gates, along paths such as Indian Ridge, or Fountain or Spruce
avenues, near the historic core of the place. Many have not focused on newer spots where burial options have multiplied. In
1973, the old Receiving Tomb overlooking Auburn Lake was
torn out. In its place was built the Auburn Court crypts. A
meditation space overlooks the lake, and the back of the rose
granite and concrete crypts faces off of Indian Ridge. Personally, I do not warm to the place; I tend to skirt by it quickly.
But newer crypts are more inviting and fit into the landscape
more successfully, while providing high density interments.
The idea of above-ground burials was new to the Boston area.
Auburn Court was so popular that additional garden crypts
were built in 1984, notably the Willow Court crypts set on the
far southeast side of the cemetery.

Even more impressive are the nearby Memorial Park graves above Willow Pond, with markers that are flush with the ground and, more recently, family names that have been carved into a stone wall that gently curves near the edge of the quiet water. Above, on a hillside, is the notable and impressive 1981 Willow Pond Knoll sculpture by Richard Duca, which sweeps up in a dramatic gesture, an evocative sail-like swoop that dominates the area. Low spiral walls were added later, with more space for names and future interments.

The newest memorial landscape, Birch Gardens, was installed in 2008 and designed by Boston landscape architect Craig Halvorson. This meditative site deliberately echoes many previous eras of burial design, in a modern cast; it features a reflecting pool, granite benches, and nine large sculpted panels, seven feet high, all connected. It is a complex, yet tranquil, design, and it offers every possible burial option imaginable. There can be upright grave markers over caskets or urn burials, and cremated remains can be interred without an urn. The walls have quickly filled with the names of those remembered here. Though it nestles on the far south end of the property, it is an attractive new locus of appeal for those who wish to seek it out. The space seems to combine every possible feature of Mount Auburn without becoming a jumble.

Halvorson says, "A garden woodland weaves through the space, blending classic Mount Auburn forms and surfaces: lawns, shrubs, groves of trees, granite and water...trees herald the entrances to the space and clusters of elegant, spring-flowing amelanchier trees—used for centuries in New England memorial landscapes—are scattered along the path."

But my favorite new space is Spruce Knoll. Paul Walker took me there; it is his favorite place in the redevelopment of Mount Auburn's grounds. It was a bright summer day, and as we got out of the electric cart, he said, "Many people walk right past it. That is its charm, how it is secluded." It is a heavily wooded rise, with several narrow paths that meet in a secluded inner clearing, where there are individual stone markers. Additional markers can be found around the knoll's circumference, providing space for cremated ashes.

"It is a wonderful feel, here," Walker says, praising the landscape architect, Julie Moir Messervy, who worked with the grounds crew to develop a largely evergreen and Norway spruce dense "forest" hilltop. The site makes deft use of clearing spaces that form, in effect, rooms where people can come and reflect, and be alone, unobserved. "It has its own aura, capturing the feel of Consecration Dell on a miniature scale."

I remembered the first time I was there, a year earlier—on a gray, rainy winter day, as a church member lay her mother's ashes in the center knolltop clearing—and how the three of us present had felt that, despite the weather, we were in a magical place, far from the rest of the world. The small, enclosed green space was private and yet not desolate. On this sunlit day with Walker, of course, the summer light made it all feel so different, yet that strong sheltering feeling remained, and I privately wondered if this might be a place I might want to be buried someday.

Messervy took her cues from the actual landscape she was asked to transform; seeing the tall spruce trees on the stark knoll inspired her design. Over the past twenty years, Messervy has worked on many projects at Mount Auburn, inspired by contemplative gardens from her time training as a landscape designer both here and in Japan. From Mount Auburn's "winding roads and paths, [it] felt like a large stroll garden. I was entranced."

Faced with the challenge of incorporating memorials, she decided to ring the new knoll design with tablets, and use artfully placed stones and new plantings to guide the mourner up into the shaded quiet interior enclosures. Here, ashes could be "directly poured into the earth. . . . The result is that visitors feel like they are walking through a little piece of nature, an experience that is quite different from anywhere else in the cemetery." She adds, "When you think about it, designing a space in a cemetery is built on creating a sacred trust between the designer and the person mourning a loved one. A designer has to be able to understand what the mourner is going through and make it a place that can 'hold' and honor those feelings."

All of these new areas—Willow Pond, Birch Gardens, Halcyon Garden, Spruce Knoll—reflect a sea change in how burial will continue in this new "hybrid" cemetery in a new century. David Sloane, author of *The Last Great Necessity: Cemeteries in American History*, says of these new designs: "This landscape reflects a 20th century approach to death, just as the other landscapes reflected a 19th century approach to death. This is a much more personal place to mourn your dead than the previous sections of Mount Auburn. You know where your monument is, your family knows where the marker is. . . . Gone is the 19th century sentiment of death. Here in the 20th century it is simpler, more modern and more distant." When I started to write this book, I was too entranced by the historic section to properly see that Mount Auburn, even before the Master Plan focus, was a place of layers where periods of history played off of each other in interesting and subtle ways. Now there are a new century's changes to consider, with habits and customs that continue to shift and accelerate.

(Though David Barnett seems rather cool to my idea of grave holograms. I think he will come around.)

Melting Art

We live in an age in which more and more people choose to move into their postlife without the comfort of epitaph, statuary, monument, or even small gravestone. Oddly, we seem to be heading back to a time in which our forebears were buried without outward adornment or marking—and were sometimes left virtually nameless. In my ministry, more people than ever say they simply want their ashes scattered on a beach or hillside or, if they are buried, then with the smallest of markers, often set into the turf, hardly raised at all. Yet one sees at a glance that Mount Auburn represents, with the highest artistry imaginable, a two-hundred-year phenomenon of the rise of the funereal monument, whether in the form of a crypt, statue, ornate marker, or gravestone.

The Reverend Cotton Mather went to view the grave of a ministerial colleague in 1693 and, startled at the effusive compliments carved there, remarked, "The stones in this wilderness are already grown so witty as to speak."

In the many decades to follow, speak they did, in so many ways. Cultural historian Richard E. Meyer, in the introduction to his *Cemeteries and Gravemarkers: Voices of American Culture*, maintains that few human institutions have quite the power to communicate as do our burial grounds. "Here may be found, conveniently grouped within carefully defined sacred or secular perimeters, an astoundingly revealing array of material artifacts . . . leading to a richer understanding of the history and cultural values of community, region, and nation. 'Nowhere else,' cultural geographer Terry Jordan has maintained, 'is it possible to look so deeply into our people's past.'"

Jordan quotes a student of his, who wrote him after deciding to study cemeteries that "without knowing it I had opened a whole new world for myself. Graveyards are not just a place of superstition or morbid high school pranks, but a place of cultural enrichment. No longer do I look at a stone and think—dead person! That stone conveys a life and life's love, anger, happiness, and place in family, community and society."

For centuries, the marked grave was for the aristocratic, the famous, the rich. A few others were lucky to be noted for a short generation, if at all, with most cast into the great maw of oblivion. The advent of the Romantic era, coupled with a rise in democratic sensibilities, meant that one's death could now be envisioned as worthy of note in stone, worthy of memory. A massive two-volume collection of notable graves, *Sepulchral Monuments*, was published in 1786; by the time of the 1809 publication of William Godwin's *Essay of Sepulchres*, a significant change was well underway.

To bury a body without a suitable marker was beginning to seem not just uncivilized, but unspiritual and disrespectful of the soul. Godwin proclaimed, "I am not satisfied to converse only with the generation of men that now happen to subsist; I wish to live in intercourse with the illustrious Dead of all ages. . . . I would say with Ezekiel, the Hebrew, 'Let these dry bones live!' as my friends, my philosophers, my instructors and my guides!"

Now, in a shift both democratic and capitalistic, if you had the funds you could join these remembered illustrious dead. In the early 1840s, the publication of books offering many monument designs made it easy to envision one's marker. Creative efforts by stone carvers and artists opened up the cemetery to this burgeoning new field, and soon families were quietly in competition to leave behind the most notable, striking monuments imaginable for their beloved. Most markers, of course, remained small, tasteful—but they rose up and, adorned with engraved signs, symbols, and suitable sentiments in their epitaphs, marked this ground for what they hoped would be eternity.

Human nature being what it is, monuments became larger, more complex, more and more adorned with urns, columns, obelisks, carved plants, crosses, angels, sleeping children, and, as you can see in Mount Auburn today, faithful dogs. Common New England stone became more expensive marble that was polished and dressed, and then came costly Italian Carrara marble for detailed and precise figurative sculpture. The Victorian cult of death was changing cemeteries; they went from simply marking individuals' lives to providing what could only be called remarkable, innovative landscapes of outdoor art, a garden sculpture museum.

Christian symbolism was commonly employed in tomb and marker decoration, of course, but it was striking how quickly, in the former land of the Puritans, the "residents" of Mount Auburn lay under marble and stone that was embossed and engraved with classical Greek and ancient Egyptian iconography. As Catharine Arnold notes, the monuments themselves proclaimed a classical influence, "with broken columns signifying a life interrupted. . . . Urns draped with a cloth indicated that the deceased was head of the household, while pyramids, inspired by the Egyptian craze, were said to prevent the devil from lying on the grave."

Today, it is hard not to be touched by the vast array of grave markers filling the grounds, their diversity and, at times, even the creative touches truly serving to make the dead somehow present, more vivid. Yet it is also not hard to see what the critics of this movement had in mind when they condemned the growing cost, the occasional ostentation and gracelessness, and the confusing jumble of styles all over the artistic map—Doric, Corinthian, Egyptian, Italianate, primitive American Colonial, Gothic, and Modern minimalistic.

The English architect Augustus Pugin referred to "that vile and pagan upstart, sepulchral Baroque" and wrote dimly of modern cemetery decoration as "something associated with great Egyptian lodges and little shabby flower-beds, joint stock companies and immortelles, dissent, infidelity, and speculation." I suspect Pugin never stepped foot into Mount Auburn, but Bigelow must have shuddered to read the influential Pugin's educated guess that these newfangled cemeteries would have an "entrance gateway . . . selected for the grand display of the company's enterprise and taste, as being well calculated from its position to induce persons to patronize the undertaking by the purchase of shares or graves."

One way or the other, the onslaught of successive seasons is going to take its toll on any gravestone, and it hardly matters how much is spent or what symbolism is employed in the design of its message. As bones molder, so too do stones crumble and erode. The deepest engraving will eventually be ground smooth by rain and wind into illegibility, and the most ornate statuary will be melted by acid rain and snow and New England salt sea breezes. This is the way of things of course: the lichen-covered greening old stone harkens back to Romantic imagery of the old churchyard. In a special landscape predicated on decay, this was the attractive outer display of the presiding principle at work. There is nothing as appealing as an old monument under siege by time, covered by flowering vines and rimmed by moss.

The instinct to preserve one's name was inherently a losing cause, a futile gesture that nature would handle in good time. Still, there was also an equally strong instinct to try—to prop up a stone broken off, to re-engrave obliterated letters, to keep a marker that "we were here" findable for as long as possible.

This is why we treat these stones with such care, such devotion, and preserve them as best we can. It is a lost cause we give our hearts to. But our forebears knew this too, and the writer Thomas Browne in the seventeenth century noted that even the most impressive stone would be legible and "tell the truth scarce forty years." When Godwin wrote of monuments, he noted the truth that "ordinary tombstones are removed much after the manner the farmer removes the stubble of this year's crop that he make room for the seed of the next."

What we employ to symbolize eternity is itself perishable.

But then, all art is perishable, even if artists are motivated by the illusion that they are making themselves immortal. And now, Mount Auburn has outdoor collections on par with a museum, according to the United States government. This would have made the founders quite happy; in always dreaming big, they had the idea early on that people should come and stroll on the grounds to be edified not only by Nature, but by tasteful art. First the Egyptian Gateway, then Washington Tower (in honor of the greatest founder of them all), and then the Gothic chapel with its ornate stained glass.

But Bigelow did not wish to stop there. In addition to the honor extended to Washington, there was the notion that four massive statues should be placed within the chapel, each honoring some aspect of our emerging American culture. After some thought, it was decided: for law, they would salute their own past president, Justice Story; for the colonial period, John Winthrop; for the revolution, James Otis; for the early republic, John Adams. All four statues were commissioned and all were eventually delivered and displayed in the old chapel—but by the time they were relocated to the new administration buildings, it was clear that there would never be room or resources to keep them on display.

So the great statues were given to Harvard, where they reside today, though separated. I remember years ago seeing the Winthrop and Adams statues in the Annenberg room at Harvard's Memorial Hall, and I take it on credit that Harvard Law School appreciates Story, and Sanders Theatre enjoys hosting Otis. One oddity of the short-lived venture was the fact that Justice Story's statue was fashioned by his son who, when commissioned by Mount Auburn, had never actually trained as a sculptor. William Wetmore Story left the law, went to Italy, and hastily studied the ancient art. Not only did he create a creditable image of his father, but he later became a renowned American artist. This indulgence was not merely a sentimental gesture—it shows how few American sculptors there were to choose from.

The story, however, opens up a new vista of appreciation of Mount Auburn. There are more than sixty thousand monuments here, and some are of national importance as works of fine art. The garden also happens to be an outstanding outdoor museum of commemorative art; many of the monuments are so precious that it hurts even to think about their ultimate fate. Acid rain and snow, and the freeze-thaw cycles of tough New England winters, will eventually, someday, melt this stone art.

Not before its time, however, as a recent $92,000 stewardship grant to document, assess, research, and photograph thirty of the cemetery's most significant monuments will help lay the groundwork to conserve these often fragile and evocative artifacts. Already on the Mount Auburn website is a series of short videos detailing the painstaking work it takes to preserve something like the Binney monument—by all accounts, the most valuable and beautiful funerary monument in America. (For me, it gives Henry Adams's memorial to his wife, Clover—in Rock Creek Park in Washington, DC—a run for its haunting value.) This masterpiece by American artist Thomas Crawford, carved in 1847, shows along its back a male soul ascending upward. Delicate drapery enfolds the figure. A pensive female figure carved along the front of the monument carries an urn. With draped cloth of marble uniting the whole edifice, the total effect is breathtaking, even factoring in more than 165 years of wear. "It is without question one of the finest and most important funerary monuments in the United States," says Lauretta Dimmick, former assistant curator for sculpture at Boston's Museum of Fine Arts.

It is the only monument here designated an American Treasure by the National Trust for Historic Preservation, and it is not hard to see why. It is also not hard to see the pressing need for intervention, both to shore up the monument itself and to halt any further damage. Cleaning is a precarious task; it involves applying mild detergent with just a basic toothbrush and hoping, as one brushes the sugaring marble surface, that you ease away the dirt and not the fragile surface itself. (Harsher chemicals used years ago have been abandoned for causing more harm than good.) A laser treatment is also applied to remove black gypsum deposits. With utmost delicacy, soft lime mortar was eased into the fine cracks. After this, a chemical "consolidant" was applied to the stone, to help strengthen the entire monument. The surfaces, though impossible to return to their perfection, are smoother now, and have been returned to the soft cream color of the original Italian Carrara marble.

All this—and only one monument conserved! The task before the preservation team is mammoth and unrelenting.

Another recent "save" is the elegant Hygeia statue upon the grave of Dr. Harriot Hunt, one of America's first woman physicians. The figure of the Greek goddess representing health and hygiene is itself in need of repair. Its hands have eroded and its features have been smoothed away by time. Recent conservation work will allow this rare work to survive another century. Not only is the statue graceful, and the commission significant in honoring an important medical figure, but the work was carved by a remarkable artist whose story needs to be recovered.

Edmonia Lewis was not only one of the first women of color to become a renowned sculptor (though astonishingly few of her works survive), she was one of the first to train and work throughout her career in Rome, which was then the center for training in the profession. With an African American father and a Chippewa (Ojibwa) mother, Lewis forged past all limitations and obstacles (including being asked to leave Oberlin College) to fashion a strong career. Pope Pius IX visited her studio and blessed it. However, she told Lydia Maria Child, "Some praise me because I am a colored girl, and I don't want that kind of praise." Her skill, even in the eroded form of Hygeia, is clear.

There are many remarkable monuments here at Mount Auburn, but there is one that nearly everyone visits, and it is the grandest and most imposing of all. The Mary Baker Eddy monument's stately reflection shimmers upon the surface of Halcyon Lake. Eddy was the only woman of her era to rival

Isabella Stewart Gardner in her dramatic alteration of Boston culture, but the two women could not have had more opposing personalities (though Eddy rivaled Gardner in the ability to irritate and provoke people). The Christian Science church Eddy left behind when she finally surrendered to the imperative of mortality succeeded in powerfully immortalizing her memory.

Both Eddy and Gardner left great and imposing monuments; in Eddy's case, an entire American religion. The late Peter Gomes once gave an address titled "The Four Greatest Figures in American Religious History" and the last was Mary Baker Eddy, because she returned the feminine to the religious, and because she returned the body to spiritual consideration—her efforts were a clear forerunner to the health and spirituality movement, and the mind-body connection, so strong today. One does not have to ascribe to Christian Science to be deeply affected by her influence. She is a particularly American figure in her attempt to yoke spirit to science, to assert that one's thoughts create spiritual reality. She was a New England Transcendentalist who insisted on taking the whole thing seriously.

The vista of Eddy's memorial overlooking Halcyon Lake is probably the most graceful sight at Mount Auburn. However, it is not true—as Mount Auburn legend has it—that Eddy was buried with a telephone in her coffin. One was installed in the crypt during construction, but that hardly counts.

Call Me Trimtab

Time is a very strange thing—nothing odder. It can seem endlessly expansive, yet can go by in a flash and, according to Einstein, it is as relative as can be. In some sense, Mount Auburn's creation in historical terms can seem an eternity ago, recalling a rural, agricultural, not yet industrialized, romantic America quite far from us. On the other hand, the *Washington Post*, within a week of my writing this chapter, published a front-page headline declaring "Amazing But True: America Is Only Four Presidents' Lives Old." In fact, I love to confound dinner guests with the announcement that President John Tyler (five presidents before Lincoln) has two living grandchildren. They immediately Google it to discover, yes—indeed he does. (This was the case as of early 2015—it can't go on forever.) This seems impossible, probably because the yawning abyss of the Civil War so obscures our history, which is divided into pre- and post-war times.

I happily discovered Margaret Fuller in divinity school, and she immediately became a powerful heroine to me, but to my college contemporaries of forty years ago, her grand-nephew Buckminster Fuller would have been a much more obvious, almost ubiquitous, hero. He was everywhere: lecturing on college campuses, popping up on magazine covers, appearing on popular talk shows. He was not a smooth or fluent writer, but he had a knack for phrases that stuck, and few bookstores would not have been filled with titles alluding to "Spaceship Earth," "synergy," and "geodesic dome construction." Fuller intended to change the world. Even if his inventions were later seen to be impractical or, in the case of his geodesic domes, prone to leaking, his actual engineering skills did not matter: he accomplished his goal of making the world see our planet as precious and fragile—a place that could be either saved or destroyed, as we chose. He was an optimist who proclaimed, like his great-aunt before him, that a new manifestation was at hand. And no one envisioned it quite as effectively as Buckminster Fuller.

When I realized that "Bucky" Fuller was buried only a short distance from Margaret's cenotaph and the Fuller family lot, it occurred to me not only that the two nicely tie together eras seemingly far apart, but that they were the ideal people to help make clear that—despite appearances—we are not actually so far from the time of Mount Auburn's founders.

If ever there was a throwback to the time of Emerson, Thoreau, and Margaret Fuller, it was Bucky, a man whom author Arthur C. Clarke called the first engineer saint. Buckminster Fuller was a designer who was also poet and prophet, and he was certainly a modern Transcendentalist.

Emerson called America's sense of its emergent self "the American newness," and no one embodied these new ideas as fully as his radical friend Margaret Fuller did. The young Buckminster Fuller admired her, and he grew up with family stories of her. Into our own time, her descendant Buckminster symbolized the full turn of the wheel, the survival of a peculiarly American self-confidence and urge to re-envision, to remake, the world. In fact, under the verbal onslaught of Bucky Fuller—renowned for his two-hour talks made without notes—the Emersonian note was revived and renewed. Bucky took seriously the words of Emerson, who said, "He is placed in the center of things, and a ray of relation passes from every other being to him."

Fuller gave us much more than the geodesic dome and the word *synergy*. He gave us a guided tour of the universe as architect, engineer, and poet; in his own words, he was "a comprehensive anticipatory design-science explorer." As he said before his death: "I am a publicity agent for the universe."

Fuller is buried with his wife, Anne, above Willow Pond. He was sitting by her hospital bed as she lay recovering from an operation when he had a heart attack at age eighty-eight and died. She died quietly two days later. They rest under a modest stone, with another small marker placed above it that reads "Call me Trimtab."

Beyond echoing Melville's iconic phrase "Call me Ishmael," what could this phrase possibly mean? A good New Englander with sailing experience would know that a trim tab is a small rudder that, in turn, can allow a great change in the main rudder's effect with surprisingly little effort (it can work on air flowing over wings, as well). It was the kind of idea Fuller loved, practical and quite real, but endlessly symbolic as well. The pressure of water on a main rudder can make it virtually impossible to turn, but the slight shift of the trim tab suddenly changes the heavy flow, and makes it possible to turn the main rudder. Fuller loved the idea of the least amount of effort creating the greatest possible effect. He thought that if he saw his life in this way—as capable of creating massive change, of literally turning the great ship of the world—that his listeners could as well.

Like Jacob Bigelow before him, Fuller had a restless polymath mind that refused to be limited—for life itself will not be so defined. Fuller talked about pollution and housing and recycling and the finiteness of our natural resources, but ultimately he really had only one subject: everything is connected, in truth, in reality. We only mess up when we ignore what happens to be irreducibly true.

After being dismissed twice from Harvard, the young Fuller found himself floundering in his early engineering career and suffering depression after the death of his first daughter. Then, at age thirty-two, he had his epiphany—a story mythical to some, taken literally by others, but real enough in its startling effect upon the rest of his life.

Standing on the shores of Lake Michigan in 1927, struggling with thoughts of suicide, he had a vision—an all-encompassing realization that he could strike a bargain with the universe, rebrand himself as "Guinea Pig B," and just see what one person might accomplish for the total good of others if he just dared to think for himself. He decided to cast his fate, to offer all he had (in a disinterested and egoless manner—though few ever confused Fuller's approach with humility per se) to change the world in an ecological way. He wanted to be useful, to see if the universe could possibly use him thus, efficiently. Calling it "egocide," he spent the rest of his life trying to be "an encouraging example of what the little, average human being can do if you have absolute faith in the eternal cosmic intelligence we call God."

The next step, after giving over his remaining life to this "little experiment," was to believe in the overarching intelligent design of the cosmos and, further, to assume that an unfettered mind will be in tune with that design. Integrity was not merely an individual moral quality—it was threaded through the universe itself, and could be trusted, uncovered, and worked with in a cooperative fashion. When he spoke of design, it was this integrity he was attempting to tap into.

When he spoke of synergy, he was referring not only to

energy that moves through space and time, but pointing to an idea that we (and particularly scientists busy investigating the smaller and smaller elements of matter) often miss—that the whole is always greater than the sum of its parts. Breaking life down into its components is useful, but often misses the essential truth of reality: that these component parts fuse into something not only greater than those parts, but something almost always unforeseen, almost unimaginable, yet part of the design. Fuller delighted in talking about this emergent quality and made it an essential part of his ecological vision.

It is easy to call Fuller nothing more than a great cosmic conversationalist—a carnival barker for old Emersonian ideas, a mystic who talked a good engineering game but couldn't back it up with results. There is truth to this. But it misses his usefulness to us, his actual Guinea Pig B-ness. At the time of his death, Fuller had the longest listing in the history of *Who's Who in America*, held dozens of copyrights and patents, and maintained a travel itinerary that would have killed a younger man. Yet this was nothing compared to his uncanny ability to communicate both danger and hope—that Spaceship Earth was imperiled, and that our minds were made of the same stuff as the comprehensive design of all that is.

Please worry, but don't succumb to despair. Be trusting, but be willing to dare reality to make something of you. The intelligence and integrity of the universe happens to be in you. The problem is we so seldom trust it. And the key to his life was this: believe what you like, but your life is only true to "pattern integrity" when your actions align with this higher, emergent design. As he said of himself, "I seem to be a verb."

Verbose? Wordy? A reviver of New England Yankee idealism? Well, yes. But in a world where Spaceship Earth is heating up faster than our brains seem to be able to process, Fuller's new manifestation may well be more pressing, and prescient, than it was even in his own lifetime. We may never live in geodesic domes, or drive his three-wheeled Dymaxion cars, but the instruction of turning that trim tab could not come too soon. There are hundreds—thousands—of reasons to visit Mount Auburn, but after coming to know this garden well through years of acquaintance, I cannot think of a better reason than to stand before that epitaph, and wonder.

The Experimental Garden

The literary critic Van Wyck Brooks is not read much anymore, which is a shame as his gentle, mocking style is
still a delight. In his book *Indian Summer*, he details the slow,
sleepy decline of Boston culture from the great ferment of
its antebellum years, when the Transcendentalist dream held
sway over Yankee imaginations. It was as if the Civil War
had somehow sapped its essential energies: "Boston was left to
gather up its relics, with a feeling that its forbears had had 'all
the fun.' . . . Last things were in order now, and all the Boston
men could do, or all they thought they could do, was to bury
the dead. Mount Auburn was becoming over-crowded."

The early beauty of the landscape had been marred and
overwhelmed by the custom of enclosing small family lots
with ornate black iron fencing, and the charm of the place had
been overdomesticated and tamed. The staid state of Mount
Auburn became a potent symbol of New England's newly
stunted self-consciousness, a sense that its better days were
behind it and the nation had moved on. Edward Everett Hale
wrote of the later years of his friend James Russell Lowell,
who was nearly the last survivor of the great literary giants
of that era: "The Boston of 1840 really believed that a visible
City of God could be established here by forces which it had
at command. It was very hard in 1885 to make the Boston of
that year believe any such thing."

The excitement had faded away into respectability and a certain reputation for Brahmin death rites, the designated "Gateway to Heaven." Boston was feeling in the doldrums, and even Mount Auburn seemed tired, constricted by choking iron fencing and concrete curbing around family lots. In the Gilded Age, death was all too evident in Mount Auburn's sedate precincts. It was now a proper place to slumber, no longer a repository of a young nation's ideals.

Peter Gomes used to delightedly read an anonymous satirical poem of the perfect life, in which a "true Bostonian" approaches heaven and lists his credentials, including having been born in Boston, educated in its best schools, having a pew in Trinity Church and a summer home in Nahant. The poem continues: "I own a villa, lawn, arcades / And last a handsome burial lot / In Mount Auburn's hallowed shades."

St. Peter thinks a bit, then replies, "Go back to Boston, friend . . . / Heaven isn't good enough for you." It was all too, too comfortable.

A gently mocking, and ultimately tragic, depiction of upper-class Boston life in the early part of the last century is the enduring masterpiece *The Late George Apley* by John P. Marquand (a fine writer who financed his serious novels by writing a long series of best-selling Mr. Moto thrillers under a different name). Mount Auburn makes an appearance as a resonate symbol of the decline of the Brahmin class. Marquand knew of what he wrote; although he often felt like an outsider as a student at Harvard, he in fact was born of New England aristocratic stock, a great-nephew of Margaret Fuller and cousin of Buckminster Fuller.

His character George Apley is a man trapped by rigid codes of self-restraint and ancestral Beacon Hill pieties. His tragedy is that he essentially surrenders a potentially happy existence to obey those constraints. As World War I nears, amid all the death and eventual social upheaval one could imagine, Apley is caught up in a family dispute over the large family lot at the cemetery. On an afternoon motoring jaunt, he swings by Mount Auburn to inspect plantings at the family lot. But to his considerable consternation, he sees that a distant relative, not part of his "particular branch" of the family, has had the audacity to be buried in his section. He sends off a letter to these relatives, barely able to contain his shock: "I cannot conceive what prompted you to allow Cousin Hattie to occupy this spot. Not only do I think she should not be there, but also her pink granite headstone with the recumbent figure on top of it, which I suppose represents an angel, makes a garish contrast to our own plain, white marble stones."

Apley demands that Cousin Hattie be exhumed forthwith and moved to another slope nearby. He adds, in defense of the immediate need of removal, that "I do not agree with you that it is too late to do anything about it. When the subway was built under Boston Common a great many bodies were exhumed from the old graveyard there and again buried."

Marquand uses the symbol of what Mount Auburn had come to represent—its status and elite sense of class sequester (even from others within that class) as a rich evocation of just how far people's sensitivities can be separated from simple humanity, and how far Mount Auburn had drifted away from its democratic origins.

But Indian summers are deceiving. Just when you think you know the lay of the land, the temperature shifts and the seasons revert to their natural order. In the presidency of Oakes Ames, which began in 1934, many of the lot fences were happily removed (those that remain are being kept and preserved in good order, to preserve a precious "layer" of historical features), and a bounteous planting of new trees recovered some of the old feel of the grounds, especially after the disastrous effects of the Great New England Hurricane of 1938. But it was not until the late 1980s that, unexpectedly, Mount Auburn entered a time of resurgence—indeed, a real renaissance.

In Justice Story's consecration address, he notes clearly the intent of the founders: "The Legislature of this Commonwealth, with a parental foresight, has clothed the Horticultural Society with authority . . . to make a perpetual dedication of it, as a Rural Cemetery or Burying-Ground, and to plant and embellish it with shrubbery, and flowers, and trees, and walks, and other rural ornaments."

It has taken more than a century to get back to this aspect of its early mission. The presidential leadership of William Clendaniel, who ordered a massive rethink called the Master Plan, has completely changed the feel and energy of this American landmark. No longer is Mount Auburn a place that sleeps a lost dream—it is up and about, reclaiming the visionary reform instincts that gave it birth in the first place.

Clendaniel drove home a sense that Mount Auburn needed to wake up, to claim all its past glories and return to its primal, first mission. Now his successor, David Barnett, a horticulturalist by training, is building on the Master Plan's success to move past this historical recovery and into territory that Dearborn dreamed of—the whole cemetery as a place of ecological experimentation and green burial reform. When I started this book, I thought Mount Auburn was, at best, a kind of strange cultural museum, but it turns out it is an experimental garden, and an increasingly radical one at that.

Mount Auburn's influence on landscape architecture and the design of gardens is subtle, but real—Transcendentalism is found in more than literary anthologies; it is in gardens all around us. In *American Eden*, garden historian Wade Graham looks at the impact of post–World War II landscape artist Daniel Kiley and his desire to "build landscapes of clarity and infinity, just like a walk in the woods." The Boston-raised, Harvard-trained designer spoke of his work "as if he were an ecologist: 'landscape architecture should be a walk in the woods; it should have that sense of mystery and perpetual growth.'"

Kiley often quoted Emerson's observation that "nature who abhors mannerisms has set her heart on breaking up all style and tricks." There was a spiritual dimension to Kiley's work: "I am always searching for the purest connection to that which holds us all together—we can call it spirit or mystery; it can be embodied by descriptions of the universe or of religion; it takes the form of sacred geometries and infinitesimal ecologies."

Isamu Noguchi, another influential landscape designer as well as a renowned sculptor, also brought this spiritual dimension into his work. His designs intentionally echoed nature's artless curves and sweeping forms. They were hardly artless, but precise, ordered, stark, and minimal. This long tradition, which extends so fruitfully into our own times, is, as Graham concludes, a "new pastoral urbanism." It provides "ground for hope, that now, more than four hundred years into the experiment, we Americans have come close to reconciling the contradictions of our existence—living in cities in the midst of a tantalizing wildness, a garden of possibility."

That hope, even in an era on the edge of ecological pain and disruption, is exactly what Bigelow and Dearborn had in mind so long ago. Mount Auburn, from the minute New Englanders took to the trolley to flock to her groves, was "pastoral urbanism" at its most hopeful.

And although the conception of what constitutes such an urban garden at Mount Auburn has shifted often, and with great and wide-ranging effect on the landscape itself, the essential mission has not—and in recent years, it has only been even more consciously reclaimed. Never, since Dearborn and his concept of a great experimental garden were essentially rejected in the late 1830s, has Mount Auburn been more of a place of pastoral innovation.

In hearing this, I asked Dennis Collins (whose job title of horticultural curator is one I have never before encountered) if this effort represented a kind of forensic horticulture—historical recapturing of a long-ago landscape. "At the dell, yes—but what we are really trying to do is see the entire landscape through time," Collins replies. "The hard work that went into the Master Plan showed us that we have a complex interweaving of layers, one kind of horticultural landscape standing next to a very different time period and layout. We can't make all of the place like it was in the 1830s, nor would we want to. The grounds then hadn't been clear-cut, the hills were steeper, the water areas in some places marshy. Perhaps the reason it was sold by George Brimmer was that all these things had made the land difficult to farm.

"Another area of creative effort is the 'new' wildflower

meadow that adorns the hillsides surrounding Washington Tower—quotes around that word *new*, because one thing I have learned is that landscape design and development takes enormous patience," Collins says. "A project can take months to conceive, then a year to find the funding for, then a time of planting, and then years of fine-tuning, adjustment, and a general holding of one's breath to see if any of it takes hold—discovering if the growing, living reality bears any resemblance to the initial idea and the planting blueprint."

After this meadow garden project was planted in 2007, the blooming results clearly satisfied visitors, who seemed to accept it as not only a pleasant and restful scene but, most importantly, as something that seems to have been there all along naturally. It satisfies the migrating birds and animals who need this particular kind of landscape; the wildflower meadow creates a habitat that did not previously exist within the cemetery, and one that is, unfortunately, growing scarcer by the day across New England. Collins proudly recounts, "Our wildflower meadow consists of over forty different types of native grasses and wildflowers and shrubs that are represented by more than fifteen thousand individual plants." What he does not say is that this kind of horticultural diversity requires long and backbreaking work. None of this is cheap, or easy.

On a summer day, as you climb to the high point of Washington Tower, you can see, on most days, the curve of the Charles River winding below and the tall horizon of Boston skyscrapers. The bank of wildflowers shimmers in the high breezes that usually cool the summit. With this project clearly in hand, Barnett, Walker, and Collins now are looking elsewhere to fulfill challenges from the old Master Plan.

As Barnett says, "We have been working on this for over

fifteen years, and it will be the next director who will see it finally finished."

The meadow of wildflowers is a lovely idea, but it is only part of a larger effort to reduce—plot by plot, lawn by turf area—exposed grass expanses that constantly need to be mowed and groomed, replacing them with a mixture of more natural tall grasses and flowers. Such transformations save a great deal of money compared with maintaining the old large lawns, but more importantly they are so much more hospitable to birds attracted to tall grasses, and to an array of insects, butterflies, and small mammals. It is an ecological win-win, and though there is a long way to go, every small victory like the wildflower meadow saves money and workers' time, and makes Mount Auburn more sustainable.

Collins reflects on the history of the shifting landscape he works on.

> By the 1850s, they were cutting, cutting, reducing the trees by thirty percent. So, no, looking at the old etchings, we don't want to go back in time, make every plant the same. In fact, it was good in the years before the Civil War, when early dark woodlands had become cheerful, sunnier. On the other hand, in the Victorian era, they enclosed plots with iron fencing and had intricate flowerbeds all over. It became a cluttered landscape, even with more open lawns. We want to keep some of that, but mostly, we want to return to a naturalistic look far from that Victorian style. We want a good mixture of styles, layered, and most of all, a lot less lawn. If I have any goal, and it's a hard one to achieve, it is to reduce turf in many areas. We don't want to return to the love-of-lawn period.

Barnett says the vision of the founders is still theirs. What made the place beautiful and inspirational generations ago remains very much in place, though so much has changed in time and circumstance. "They started with the intent of creating an experimental garden, and though it did not last long, that idea is now back, at the very heart of all we are trying to do here. The old vision is our mission." This is not just rhetoric, but an investment of millions of dollars for a comprehensive overhaul. Construction of the massive new greenhouse, concentration on organic techniques in every aspect of operations, creation and reclamation of wildlife habitats, and, most importantly, radical reconception of death through the incorporation of green burial ideas—all are making the place truly "experimental" again. The staff is learning to do without fertilizer and implementing cutting-edge practices; staff members serve as national leaders both in educating the public and in working with cemetery and arboretum colleagues all over the country to transform what it means to be a historical rural park cemetery. "We are both circling back and moving forward. We are trying to be proactive leaders."

There is always a challenge in trying to preserve a historic property. No one expects Colonial Williamsburg to suddenly become a leader in windmill technology, or Sturbridge Village to transform itself into a world peace center. It is hard enough to just maintain what you are in a fast-moving culture that is not always sympathetic to such efforts. This is what makes Barnett's sense of commitment to making Mount Auburn an ecological beacon—not just to other cemeteries, but to the nation at large—so interesting. But he does not see it as daring, or a reach. He sees it as a fulfillment of the vision that was handed down to his staff and to a dedicated backup array of local board members and volunteers.

Of course, it is a challenge to maintain Mount Auburn

as the special place it is, but Barnett prefers to see its future as more a challenge to our culture at large. "If we can shift people's thinking about the environment, as well as preserve this particular landscape, then we can be teachers to everyone who walks into this place, and beyond."

He wants a clear focus on what he calls "the green team"—to move aggressively in all departments to demonstrate advancements in sustainability, in wildlife preservation, in landscape design, in green burials, and in what he calls, pun probably not intended, being "leaders on the ground." Something as small as being able to bury a body in a simple shroud is a symbol of so much more; natural burials here can begin to change far more than attitudes toward death and dying, they can influence attitudes about the very sustainability of life—of wildlife, flora, water, the world we have inherited. History is important here, but that history, through the influence of Bigelow and his partners, tells Barnett that simply maintaining Mount Auburn is not enough, and not what the founders truly had in mind.

Though his approach is rooted in old American practicality and sound scientific research, Barnett is part of a long line of botanists who were affiliated with Mount Auburn, including Bigelow and Gray. He notes that the previous botanists' strong sense of following the lead of the past means this is not just about good practices or better techniques. "They created a place of rare beauty and peacefulness. We are aware of that. Everything we do here and in the future has to respect and value nature itself: the trees, the birds, the grasses and flowers—the salamanders!—and all that we have responsibility to care for here. Their primary vision was inspirational, and we have to work hard to inspire. In respecting the dead, and in respecting the landscape, we understand there is something deeply spiritual going on, and always has been."

Barnett is a scientist, a detail guy, so he won't go further than this. He sees Mount Auburn as the nonsectarian, nondenominational, interfaith, and transfaith place it was from its founding, but he is unabashed in seeing its mission as something close to mystical. It is just that he sees this spiritual dimension in terms of the things he deeply loves, and those happen to be trees most of the time.

David Barnett loves all plants, but certain trees just appeal to him, and they are mostly ancient and really, really tall. Though he was never trained in the field, the historical aspect of Mount Auburn appeals to him more and more—especially as it concerns those trees. There are more than five thousand trees on the site, and Barnett proudly points to the impressive fact that nearly thirty of the trees predate the founding—they were part of George Brimmer's "Sweet Auburn," where Harvard students used to stroll and locals picnicked in the lush woodlands.

Those trees are mostly white and black oaks; another 180 are nearly that old. More than 150 sugar maples survive from at least the Civil War. Though not as ancient as the oaks, they are precious indeed. When an old tree shows signs of strain and looks a goner, Barnett and Paul Walker speak of it as if it were an old friend as they seek some last intervention to stave off the loss of one more.

In the course of writing a book, you never know where source materials will take you, where a stray conversation will lead. Yes, the manuscript will veer off in unforeseen ways, you can expect that—but sometimes it's more about the shifts within you. In conceiving this book, I thought I would have about equal parts Mount Auburn miniature biographies and a survey (hopefully lively) of burial customs. Instead, I find I have recovered an early love of birds, reconnected with early American writers I hadn't read in thirty years, and discovered a greening world I thought I appreciated—but learned I knew essentially nothing about.

While the staff of Mount Auburn was kindly attempting to orient me and make me comfortable, I had so massively far to go. I was starting from innocent, if not ignorant, eyes for all flora. Since I am a bookish person, nothing has surprised or enlightened me more than encountering the novelist John Fowles's eponymous essay in his book *The Tree* (with photographer Frank Horvat's haunting photos) and discovering how it has affected the way I see and experience Mount Auburn. To trail behind Barnett or Collins or Walker on the grounds is to quickly know all you don't know—not just Latin names, but any name, any label. My eyes blur, my ignorance inwardly shored up by a self-righteous defense that I happen to see the whole, the gestalt of the ground, and that I'm not the kind of person to get lost in the particulars.

The more I learn to love Mount Auburn, the more I realize how shaky and forlorn that reassurance is, but Fowles helps me justify it to some limited extent. He writes how the early Victorian mania for classification and rigor was not an unalloyed positive. He focuses first on the way in which human beings, in a scientific mode or not, tend to center on the individual, the singular, the one tree. He prefers to focus on "the complex internal landscapes they form when left to themselves," and "the canopy and exterior wall of leaves, and beyond the individual."

In other words, we like to look at a tree, but trees are in fact not singular beings. They are copses, forests, terrains: "We feel, or think we feel, nearest to a tree's 'essence' (or that of its species) when it chances to stand like us, in isolation. . . . Far more than ourselves they are social creatures, and no more natural as isolated specimens than man is as a marooned sailor or hermit." In turn, trees in "social" gathering form a complex environment with birds, animals, insects, and the smallest of organisms—the "whole experience of the wood."

Second, wrote Fowles, to name and label a plant is to think we understand it and have solidly placed it in the scope of the natural world, but perhaps all we have done is focus so sharply that we cease to see at all. Fowles thinks back to his youthful enthusiasms as an amateur naturalist and wonders if all he was doing was treating nature "as some sort of intellectual puzzle, or game, in which being able to name names and explain behaviorisms—to identify and to understand machinery—constituted all the pleasures and the prizes."

Yet it is hard, in truth, to justify the sense that swimming in ignorance is an elevated way to go; that Barnett's evident love and intimate knowledge is some kind of scientific distancing and intellectual game. Thoreau knew the name of everything he viewed and touched, and you can't read him out of the Transcendentalist fold—in fact, he demonstrates that keen apprehension and appreciation is the way to sense the divinity in all things. It is in the particular that the whole may be revealed.

I am a very amateur painter, and I suspect my blobby green trees would look transformed, perhaps transfigured, if I in fact knew the structure of the very leaves I was painting, the way nature instructs branches to lift off the trunk, the way roots grasp and claw the ground. Yes, I have to learn to see not one, but the many—though one particular tree might be my access point to the whole. And if I learn that the Japanese *Stewartia* is known for its ornate palette of thin brown striping in crazed vertical quilt patterns, which Barnett pointed out to me as a great bark among barks, then I am actually seeing it sharpen out of my previous blur.

Whether I know the names of the trees or not, Fowles helps me see why Mount Auburn is a haunted, holy site. For decades, I had assumed that the monuments themselves created this sense in me. Now that I have prowled the grounds in all seasons, I am at the beginning of a new apprehension—that yes, it may be the gestalt, the totality of the landscape that is affecting me, but also, and late in the game, I was simply not understanding the effect of the massive stands of trees gathered here. I was experiencing something powerful—an evocation of divinity—but not fully understanding what I was in fact responding to.

Trees are driven by more than sap—they are engines of massive power and towering, mysterious life that far outlasts our limited spans. Fowles writes,

> Even the smallest woods have their secrets and secret places, their unmarked precincts, and I am certain all sacred buildings, from the greatest cathedral to the smallest chapel, and in all religions, derive from the natural aura of certain woodland or forest settings. In them we stand among older, larger and infinitely other beings, remoter from us than the most bizarre other non-human forms of life, blind, immobile, speechless.

In other words, I had thought the signs of mortality were what gave resonance to the landscape at Mount Auburn. It turns out, I may have had it all backwards: perhaps the woodlands framed the graves with this religious aura, and learning these trees—the way they stand among one another, the way they rise up, live, and die—is a path to an experience of the holy I never expected, desperately needed, and yet had somehow always had access to, as we all do.

In 1948, the naturalist Henry Beston ended his book *North-ern Farm* with the declaration, "What has come over our age is an alienation from Nature unexampled in human history." These sentiments have been only more painfully observed in the decades since, but they were hardly unnoted even in Emerson's time. We Americans are people of a strange paradox—we see divinity in Nature and at the same time are incredibly fervent in reining in its power over us. We wish to be one with these eternal cycles, even as we divorce ourselves more and more from their display and vividness. If it is true, as Thoreau wrote near the end of his life, that "it is in vain to write on the seasons unless you have the seasons in you," then we are doing much more than denying Nature's power, we are denying any true sense of our actual self.

Oakes Ames certainly deserves credit, according to Collins, for his ambitious horticultural program, extending into the late 1960s, which echoed advancements at the nearby Arnold Arboretum, particularly after the destruction caused by the hurricane of 1938, when "we lost twenty percent of the trees, over nine hundred of them." The replanting effort was ambitious and involved large investment. Still, despite this effort to enhance the natural beauties of Mount Auburn, Collins says that from the 1920s to the '80s, the place fell into a "sleepy phase, with low public interest, cruising at low gear. Then, in the 1990s, we woke up. We invited the public back, and we decided to make ambitious landscape improvements. The Master Plan kicked it off, of course—to enhance the scale of the projects we were willing to take on. The entire landscape was now seen as a series of zones, where we could make improvements to each area. More than fifteen years later, the visitor will perceive the improvements, even if they can't specifically name them."

And what is the long-term hope?

"We won't completely abandon the highly ornamental styles of the past you still see in some areas," Collins says, "but overall, we want to return to a naturalistic parkland rural style where we can. We want to have beautiful trees, wonderful specimens of character and vitality. It is satisfying to see some of your work begin to reach a certain age. Often, of course, you're planting for a time you will never see, twenty years or more beyond. And it's a moving target, as well, where you are always dealing with the unexpected—plans are fine, but fires and hurricanes have to get dealt with.

"Of course," Collins adds, "we do get to enjoy some short-term rewards 'on the ground level,' with shrubs, groundcovers, flower beds—all these are easier to see if they are working."

Collins pauses. It is back to turf. "But overall—if we can just get rid of grass. If you care about ecological sustainability, and we do, it is maintaining huge expanses of turf that really affects our carbon footprint. For more than a decade, we have tried to return to the naturalistic lawns, with blends of fescue grass, tall grasses, flowers—and get off pesticide treatments as well. When you can get wildflowers and tall grasses to eight inches, revive that meadow look that the early Mount Auburn had . . ."

This is why the butterfly garden at Willow Pond and the wildflower meadow at Washington Tower are both successful experiments, and clues to the future. "When you can mix together seventy or eighty varieties of plants which work well together, are attractive, and sustainable, then you've created something that's an advancement."

Collins is a serious man, but he leans back and reflects with pleasure on the work of the last several decades. "But truthfully, the biggest contribution we can make is to inspire others. If we can inspire enthusiasm for horticulture in the public, then we are doing our job. We are here for a limited time, a drop in the bucket; it will take many generations. But we can help transform the urban experience."

The Sphinx
Bigelow Redux

Across from Bigelow Chapel stands one of the strang-
est and most weirdly moving objects in a place haunted
by hundreds of them—the graceful yet coiled intensity of a
Sphinx. Renowned Boston sculptor Martin Milmore fashioned *The American Sphinx* in 1872 from a forty-ton block of
Maine granite, but every line, every sinew of the massive lion's
body with serene woman's head was closely directed by Jacob
Bigelow.

The old doctor, who had effectively ruled over Mount Auburn for its first forty years, was rapidly losing his sight. He
realized his time was limited. He had done so much, from
the first glimmer of the rural cemetery idea—laying out the
roads and paths, designing the gate and tower and chapel, su-
pervising virtually every aspect of the ground's care, writing
Mount Auburn's first history—all this, but something was
still missing.

Dozens of new gravesites dotting the grounds testified to
the war's catastrophic losses and the nation's traumatic crisis.
Bigelow pondered how the dead could be remembered, and
how slavery's end—the result of four years of this vast violence
—could be honored as well.

He wrote four lines to be engraved, in both Latin and
English, upon the huge pedestal where the memorial would be
placed—simple words for a complex war:

American union preserved
African slavery destroyed
By the uprising of a great people
By the blood of fallen heroes

He thought of great monuments to other battles in world history, and the varied majestic images employed to portray the great questions of life, death, mortality. In the end, nothing appealed to the old man more than the ancient world's fusion of a powerful lion's body with a human face, the Sphinx.

Because Bigelow never thought small, he dreamed this memorial would be colossal and placed in the midst of a dedicated space facing the chapel—a symbol of sacrifice that could never be forgotten. To a person standing in front of it today, gazing into the far-seeing eyes of the woman's visage, Bigelow's monument seems to ask as many questions of us as humans have ever posed to the ancient Sphinx.

Thousands have asked: what does this unnervingly serene statue mean?

Although few people ever seemed able to resist Bigelow's enthusiasms, Mount Auburn's proprietors balked at the ambition of his plan and the potential cost of the great monument. Bigelow was not daunted; he went ahead anyway, commissioning Milmore to embark on the great statue project. Milmore, remembered today mostly for his soaring Union soldier memorial high in the center of Boston Common, obtained a single block of granite, "fifteen feet long, by about eight feet in height, the face alone measuring three feet in length." The massive granite block was delivered to Milmore's Tremont

Street studio in Boston by railroad, and he and his brother set to work following Bigelow's clear instructions.

Bigelow chose a woman's face, following the Greek tradition rather than the Egyptian one, which usually placed a male face upon a lion's form. In a small book, only seventeen pages long, published after his death, Bigelow wrote, "What symbol can better express the attributes of a just, calm, and dignified self-reliance than one which combines power with attractiveness, the strength of the lion with the beauty and benignity of woman?"

Milmore carved several American images into the statue to further distinguish it from the traditional classic Sphinx familiar to all, the Great Sphinx near the pyramids at Giza, Egypt. Instead of an asp, Milmore carved a small American eagle head upon the woman's regal headdress. There is an Egyptian lotus at the southern end of the Sphinx's pedestal and, facing north, an American water lily (*Nymphaea odorata*). With the four-line inscription, all these elements reinforced Bigelow's intent to "express, though imperfectly, the gratitude felt to those of our countrymen who have given their lives to achieve the greatest moral and social results of modern times."

The Civil War unleashed a force that few had anticipated. With the freeing of 3.5 million persons (a goal few had seen as attainable at the start of the conflict), something vast and difficult of expression had been loosed into the nation's psyche. Bigelow called this a "social transition a result of greater magnitude in the history of the world than were all the revolutions and conquests of the primeval East." Out of the dim past, he was bringing forth a symbol that "now looks forward to illimitable progress."

After six months, *The American Sphinx* was moved to the

cemetery for placement. Faced with such a gift, the reluctant proprietors admitted defeat, accepted the Sphinx and paid for the great pedestal and its situation in the new garden space before the chapel, though one trustee noted disquiet over the prospect that horses would be frightened at the sight.

Meanwhile, Bigelow's cataracts continued to worsen, and as he descended into blindness he would come to the cemetery just to run his hands over the completed statue—in fact, he probably never actually saw the final result. After so much personal effort by Bigelow, the great monument was installed in August 1872. He had wanted a symbol to commemorate the thousands of lives that had been sacrificed for the Great Cause, "a landmark of a state of affairs which the world has not before seen—a great, warlike, and successful nation in the plenitude and full consciousness of its power." Out of war, peace; out of death, new life.

All this he wrote in explanation, but more than a hundred years later the Sphinx remains a mysterious beast, asking more questions than she will ever answer. The curious, questing mind of the philosophically inclined doctor was stilled on January 10, 1879, seven years after *The American Sphinx* was installed, and more than forty years from his erecting his burial marker, a plain marble sarcophagus on Beech Avenue.

The Sphinx continues to exert a pull on visitors, perhaps not because it lies between animal and the human but because it occupies a liminal point touching all we know of the intensities of life. That is where she finally rests. We live the years of our days marking the seasons, but in our birth and by our dying, we are caught up in the cycle of life's energies. In the scope of one life all this is hard to see, but walking through a gentle landscape like Mount Auburn gives a sense of something greater than a short existence. As usual, Emerson got there first, as he wrote in his poem "May-Day":

> The world rolls round,—mistrust it not,—
> Befalls again what once befell;
> All things return, both sphere and mote,
> And I shall hear my bluebird's note,
> And dream the dream of Auburn dell.

EPILOGUE
A New Adam and Eve

P erhaps the most poignant monument in Mount Auburn's history is long gone, its crumbling marble replaced in 1934 by a simple granite marker. But for decades thousands of visitors flocked every year, with something approaching reverence, to sculptor Henry Dexter's small masterpiece, *Little Emily*.

The simple, life-size marble portrait depiction of a little girl lying in stillness—as if in a bed covered by a temple-like canopy and a funeral urn—touched something tender in people's hearts. Charles J. F. Binney, a rich Boston merchant, went to Dexter, a blacksmith-turned-sculptor, after the death of his four-year-old daughter. The grieving father asked if Dexter might sculpt Emily as if in sleep and Dexter agreed, completing the work in 1842.

Upon its placement, the piece struck a chord among New Englanders, who went to view it, I suspect, both for its evocation of the (sadly prevalent) mortality of children as well as for Dexter's sensitive accomplishment; he created the first life-size marble figure by an American artist. Something about the work—the entire tableau, the inscription " 'Tis but the casket that lies here— / The gem that filled it sparkles yet," the placid girl in peaceful repose, the dark overhanging trees that draped the spot in melancholy green light—made a startling impression on the minds of visitors, including one Nathaniel Hawthorne, a man not easily moved in this way.

As long as I have been writing this book, an Oscar Wilde saying has been bothering me. I think the reason it nags at me is that it feels so apropos of what I learned researching this little plot of earth: "The Book of Life begins with a man and a woman in a garden, and ends in Revelations."

Hawthorne's eerie fantasy "A New Adam and Eve," from his *Mosses from an Old Manse*, draws from this primal creation story. It reflects the religious speculations of his fellow citizens that their world was fast drawing to a close, that it was indeed a time of Revelations. The new nation was drunk with apocalypse. This is an aspect of antebellum life mostly forgotten. Boston and the new nation seethed with millennial fever, amid numerous proclamations that the end-time was near. All of Boston was on tenterhooks when religious prophet William Miller declared the end of the world. It didn't end, so a new date was announced, and eventually other more muddied and less specific end-time fantasies supplanted it. (Before you easily dismiss the Millerites—it turns out that they evolved into the quite healthy Seventh-day Adventists today).

The peculiar genius of Hawthorne was his ability to see, in this hunger for an end to history, a desire for the opportunity to begin the world all over again—apocalypse turning, and returning, to the Garden.

Hawthorne's story is, at first, an almost whimsical tale of a world where these fantasies of the end of the world have indeed come to pass, with all human life gone, all present generations disappeared ("for instance, let us conceive good Father Miller's interpretation of the prophecies to have proved true") except for a newly created couple who find themselves, without knowledge or history or understanding, wandering in the world Hawthorne's readers would have quite easily recognized. The new Adam and Eve are in Boston and, after finding a dry goods store, are clothed to begin their journey of exploration.

The story has no plot as such. The two merely wander about the sights of a forlorn, abandoned Boston—a world they have no means of comprehending. Eve exclaims, "What can these things mean? Surely I ought to know—yet they put me in a perfect maze!" They visit a church, a courtroom, the state house, a prison, a Beacon Hill mansion, and a bank, then they go to the suburbs of the great silent city. After they see the Bunker Hill monument and Harvard University, with equal noncomprehension, their long journey takes them out of the city and into the countryside, where at sunset they enter the eden of Mount Auburn, its beauty fading in the light.

"With light hearts—for earth and sky now gladden each other with beauty—they tread along the winding paths, among marble pillars, mimic temples, urns, obelisks, and sarcophagi." They move deeper into the garden of graves.

They do not know death—yet. Still, the objects adorning each spot move them, and the seed of final knowledge begins to grow. Though this dawning insight is ascribed to two creatures who are absorbing the first day of their world, I believe Hawthorne would wish us all to awaken to it, burdened by knowledge as we are: "The idea of Death is in them, or not far off. But were they to choose a symbol . . . it would be the Butterfly soaring upward, or the bright Angel beckoning them aloft, or the Child asleep. . . . Such a Child, in whitest marble, they have found among the monuments of Mount Auburn."

For the early republic, these Mount Auburn motifs evoked nothing less than a new life, in a new Eden.

There is a chilling moment near the end of *The Great Gatsby* in which narrator Nick Carraway looks back on the Long Island landscape, which has been the scene of so much violence and crushed idealism in the course of the story. Still, somehow, something magical emanates from the sight: "For a transitory enchanted moment man must have held his breath in the presence of this continent, compelled into an aesthetic contemplation he neither understood nor desired, face to face for the last time in history with something commensurate to his capacity for wonder."

It might seem odd to quote this passage so late in this book, but F. Scott Fitzgerald captures here something that I believe people experience within this small landscape, something they rarely find words for. It tugs at them—a certain sad, yet ennobling poignancy; hushed reverberations from the past. It is hard to say why this is so—why, unlike so many other hostels of mortality, this particular landscape seems so alive and, most of all, why it remains a spot "commensurate" with our sense of wonder.

The modern world does not have much room anymore for the notions of those who built Mount Auburn. Angels and cherubim mean little to us, and we are not even certain if we possess a soul. B. F. Skinner lies buried here, and his ideas of what we are truly made of—instincts and impulses and inner levers by which operant conditioning can shape our psychologies—seem more to the point than that generation's talk of eternal souls and heavenly reunions with the dead. Respect, veneration, affection—yes, we still come here to offer these to our departed, but expectation of resurrection or eternal existence?

Yet, even as we live in the wake of the modern dislocation from the spiritual beliefs that created this landscape, we are not as far away from the founders as it sometimes seems. Theologies change, scientific understandings change, circumstances shift—but what does not change is human nature. We mourn our dead, and we fear the unknown. We instinctively respond to signs of vivid life, from flashing birds to gold and russet dying leaves. Beauty tugs at us.

We too want to preserve what we know we did not create.

Yes, we are very different from Bigelow and his company, those visionaries who fell in love with this rolling landscape and decided not only to carefully shape and carve and fill it in, but also—in the most telling of all gestures—to place within it the remains of those they loved. Our customs of burial and commemoration are changing, but we understand who these people were, and because we do, we want to save what they created and built and planted.

In truth, they understood that they actually knew as little about death as today we freely admit. And yet, we yearn to believe, in the midst of our doubt, in something as beautiful as they did.

Human yearning and longing and pain and, in the end, a strange sense of triumph—these human instincts do not change, are not lost. Mount Auburn is many things—a park, a cemetery, an arboretum, an outdoor art museum, an aviary, a wildlife preserve—but it is mostly this: a place of connection where we remember, and celebrate, the vivid lives of those who came before, those whom we will join. When epitaphs and dates and, finally, names are worn away, these stones will still speak a simple truth.

We were once alive, so alive. We loved, and are loved still.

APPENDIX
The Residents—Where to Find Them

Jacob Bigelow, Beech Avenue, Lot 116

Edward Everett, Magnolia Avenue, Lot 17

Joseph Story, Narcissus Path, Lot 33

Henry Wadsworth Longfellow, Indian Ridge Path, Lot 580

Mary Walker, Camelia Path, Lot 3774

George Brimmer, Indian Ridge Path, Lot 316

Bernard Malamud, Azalea Path, Lot 10652

Margaret Fuller (cenotaph memorial), Pyrola Path, Lot 2250

Robert Gould Shaw (cenotaph memorial), Pine Path, across from Bigelow Chapel

William Ellery Channing, Greenbrier Path, Lot 678

Dorothea Dix, Spruce Avenue, Lot 4731

Amos Lawrence, Cypress Avenue, Lot 490

Charles T. Torrey, Spruce Avenue, Lot 1282

Asa Gray, Holly Path, Lot 3904

Louis Agassiz and Elizabeth Cary Agassiz, both Bellwort Path, Lot 2640

Robert Creeley, Tulip Path, Lot 1509

Charles Sumner, Arethusa Path, Lot 2447

Josephine Shaw Lowell and Charles Russell Lowell, both Fountain Avenue, Lot 323

Phillips Brooks, Mimosa Path, Lot 1288

Julia Ward Howe and Samuel Gridley Howe, both Spruce Avenue, Lot 4987

William Brewster, Larch Avenue, Lot 1099

Ludlow Griscom, Palm Avenue, Lot 7370

Peter Byus, Magnolia Avenue, Lot 3752

Harriet Jacobs, Clethra Path, Lot 4389

Benjamin Roberts, Fir Avenue, St. John Lot, Lot 4389

David McCord, Chestnut Avenue, Lot 7012

Mary Baker Eddy, Halcyon Avenue, Lot 6234

Buckminster Fuller, Bellwort Path, Lot 2669

Here are some other figures who, if this book could be twice as long, help illustrate the fascinating array of people buried here at Mount Auburn.

Oliver Wendell Holmes, Lime Avenue, Lot 2147
Though his writings are not much read today, Holmes remains an attractive and compelling figure in our literary history—an odd fate for one of America's greatest physicians, a man who saved thousands of lives with his innovative research into puerperal fever. There did not seem any area of life that his sparkling wit and insight did not touch, in the place he called "the hub of the solar system," his beloved Boston. As a young man he wrote a poem that saved the USS *Constitution* from destruction. He would later humorously de-

construct the old Calvinist system in the poem "One Hoss Shay." And he charmed the nation through years of self-satire as the "Autocrat of the Breakfast Table." Yet he was more than wit and charm, as his disturbing psychological novel *Elsie Venner* proved, to the distress of readers not ready for a little pre-Freudian realism. It seems Boston is not quite done with the good doctor; recently, on leaving the Cathedral Church of St. Paul across from the Boston Common, I saw that his poem "The Chambered Nautilus" was the inspiration for a new pediment design facing the crowds flowing along Tremont Street.

Francis Parkman, Indian Ridge Path, Lot 2919

There are other great historians buried in Mount Auburn, but none who braved and suffered more for their work than Francis Parkman. Like Richard H. Dana Jr., who went west by sail and recorded his tale in *Two Years Before the Mast*, Parkman was a Boston Brahmin who decided he would forsake the ease of Boston and go west by land. *The Oregon Trail* was a young man's book—direct, daring, and even dangerous. But Parkman was struck by a vision: that he would tell his young nation just how long this westward surge had been going on, and what a saga it was. For decades, the reclusive writer painstakingly etched out, spindly line by spindly line, this great epic across six masterpieces (in twenty volumes) and over five thousand pages—all as he steadily went blind. Often he could work only minutes a day before the blinding pain became too great. But he prevailed, and his vivid history of the clash between the French and the British to determine the fate of a continent was to be a lifetime's work—that is, when he was not busy developing more than a thousand varieties of roses.

Isabella Stewart Gardner, Oxalis Path, Lot 2900

You may come visit the grave of "Mrs. Jack" in the great Gardner vault, though her spirit dwells not there, but in the vast Italian villa she built in the Fens of Boston (near her beloved Red Sox) in the last decade of her life. The Isabella Stewart Gardner Museum is stuffed literally from carpet to ceiling fresco with the art of Europe, as selected by her advisor Bernard Berenson. Upon her death, she gave her self-museum to the city that had been alternately shocked and delighted by her wit and exuberance over the decades. The bequest came with the stipulation that nothing was to ever be moved or changed. Her soul still fills each painstakingly designed room. The delight of the house is that you still expect her to come sweeping in, ready to adjust one of her beloved masterpieces. At the cemetery she is surrounded by a close circle of Beacon Hill women whose aesthetic and artistic temperaments, like Gardner's, changed Boston forever: Annie Fields (wife of famed editor James T. Fields and later companion to the novelist Sarah Orne Jewett) and Sarah Wyman Whitman (artist and America's first female book designer). The women are gathered together again at Mount Auburn.

Winslow Homer, Lily Path, Lot 563

It has begun to dawn on art critics and historians, as well as on the thousands still instinctively drawn to his work, that Winslow Homer might well be the greatest painter of American life there has ever been. He grew up playing at Mount Auburn, in fields not far from his grave, and his instinctive feel for landscape, mountain, and seashore was primal. Few if any artists have traveled so far in their artistic careers as Homer did; he went from early black-and-white block newspaper prints to the deftest touch of watercolor and the majesty of roiling oil sketches of violent waves. In fact, his early sentimental work—a step away from the ethos of Currier and Ives—evolved into a dark, brooding, nearly existential series of works that signal what the nation as a whole had endured in his long life. His Civil War paintings made his reputation. As he grew more reclusive, more personally isolated, later paintings such as *The Gulf Stream* (in which a man stoically awaits death at sea) and *Fox Hunt* (in which the fox seems doomed under the black wing of crows) awed—and confused—his contemporaries. The self-confident energies of early America that had filled his early work became muted and, despite his still vibrant brushwork, were now calmly painted as if held under the hand of indifferent fate.

Edwin Booth, Anemone Path, Lot 3281

The thrilling and dynamic actor bestrode his time as few tragedians have before or since, remaining the only man ever to perform *Hamlet* more than a thousand times. He infused every role with grace and melancholy power, perhaps because his own personal life vied with his roles in terms of shock and regret. His famed actor father, Junius Brutus Booth, was half mad; his first wife died early in their marriage, and the second went insane; and—oh yes, his brother assassinated our most beloved president, Abraham Lincoln. He rose above it all to be called "The Fiery Star."

James Russell Lowell, Fountain Avenue, Lot 323

Like Homer, editor and poet Lowell grew up playing in the woods of the neighboring cemetery, and though he would travel the world representing his nation as a writer as well as a diplomat, in truth, he never wandered far from Mount Auburn. He joked that he and his friend Longfellow were both in a long contest toward the place. But Lowell had a serious and poignant bond with Mount Auburn; he buried his wife Maria here, and he suffered through the childhood deaths of three of their four children. His poem "The First Snowfall" describes his first daughter Blanche's Mount Auburn grave under snow. Though sentimental in the style of the "fireside" poets of the time, it is still moving. Many of his witty satires (abolitionist in sentiment) that made his reputation in his own time verge on the unreadable today, but his talents as a teacher, editor, and lively essayist still make the large-souled Lowell one of our great American men of letters. He left behind no masterpiece (with the exception, perhaps, of the hymn "Once to Every Soul and Nation," beloved by Martin Luther King Jr.) but helped create a fertile and mature literary culture in which others could flourish.

Amy Lowell, Bellwort Path, Lot 3401

Few would have predicted in the 1920s, at the height of her fame, that the impresario persona of the cigar-smoking poetess of Brookline, Amy Lowell, would in time come to eclipse the fame of all the previous renowned and respectable Lowells of Massachusetts. Her imagistic work, which startled and bemused her contemporaries, is read now with a renewed appreciation for its delicacy and power. As the title of her recent biography states, we are looking at Amy Lowell anew. She was famous as a popular reader, lecturer, and biographer of Keats. Her eleven books of poetry were greeted with, if not positive, at least riveted, attention. In her time, there was no escaping the confident assertion of the wealthy and socially elevated Amy Lowell that it was time for American poetry to employ a new style, to escape old sentimentalities and creaky high-minded rhetorical generalities. She espoused hard, clear words to create strong, lasting images in the reader's mind, in contrast to the dreary sermonizing that characterized so much of the previous generation's poetry. Although T. S. Eliot called her the "demon saleswoman" of what she called the "new poetry," her atmospheric yet precise images created interesting new modes for younger poets to follow. Love lyrics she wrote for her partner, Ada Russell, were in her time largely overshadowed by her electric platform presence, or were politely ignored, but they are steadily gaining new appreciation.

Nathaniel Bowditch, Tulip Path, Lot 1207

For those entering Mount Auburn, a sight that compels attention is the benign old bald man cast in bronze at the junction of Central and Cypress avenues. He sits brooding over his domain with globe and navigational quadrant in hand. This is Nathaniel Bowditch, who in his time was one of America's first great international heroes (and father to the lawyer mentioned earlier in this book), though few recognize his visage today. Everything about his renown was unlikely. Somehow a mild-mannered, Salem-born sea captain with a studious interest in mathematics and the stars came to be seen, along with Franklin and Jefferson, as a worldwide symbol of American ingenuity and scientific curiosity. Bowditch transformed maritime navigation with his book of calculations called *The American Practical Navigator*. He worked on the guide as he toiled on the China seas, and later while he served as director of a Boston insurance firm. It was the classic American story—genius tossed off in the midst of the hard work of getting ahead. His statue at Mount Auburn was the first life-size bronze ever cast in America.

Also buried here are Fannie Farmer, inventor of the "scientific" recipe (meaning recipes that specified measured ingredients); Arthur Schlesinger Jr., historian and Kennedy advisor (with his customary bow-tie etched on his marker); architect Charles Bulfinch; John Bartlett of quotation fame; radical journalist I. F. Stone; Harvard psychologist B. F. Skinner; and Mary Sawyer Tyler, about whom (it is said) "Mary Had a Little Lamb" was written—and on and on. As anyone who starts down the path of tracing these lively stories knows, the trail is endless. I have told only a few of these stories. And as I have tried to convey, each of these lives, famous or not, adds to the subtle yet enlivening power of the place.

ACKNOWLEDGMENTS

J.R.R. Tolkien wrote, "Not all who wander are lost," and although I have spent the last two years wandering Mount Auburn's winding paths, I have never felt lost, mainly because of the excellent and trustworthy guides who went with me every step of the way. I would like to thank them here; not only do they have my heartfelt appreciation, they deserve to have their names "engraved" in this book. From the very beginning of this project, it has truly been a collaborative effort with the Mount Auburn staff. Though errors and shortcomings remain mine alone, the truth is that any insights conveyed here are the result of team guidance and support. And when the editors of Beacon Press came on board this collaborative effort, it really took off.

Let's face it—to say that I expected writing a book about a cemetery—any cemetery—could end up being so enjoyable is a stretch.

Yet that is what happened, and I trust the book's tone reflects that inspiration and deep pleasure. Mount Auburn is simply too beautiful and vivid a place to have a gloomy book written about it. I have not shied away from the brooding reality of death, but I have tried to reflect the intent of the founders, who wished to create a space in people's lives where, even in mourning, they could feel more intensely alive. The founders invented a new kind of shared rural park landscape, and changed America. Luckily for me, the present staff of Mount Auburn effortlessly share that mission, and that daily enjoyment. I have never seen such a contented, sane, happy set of fellow workers in all my life. I hated ending this project because I have liked working among them.

The Lively Place would not exist without the original vision of Jane Carroll, vice president of development, who wondered if I would be interested in creating a general interest book, one designed to appeal not only to strong supporters of Mount Auburn, but also to the thousands of more casual visitors who flow through here each year. Not a guidebook, not a historical tome—something to explain in a clear and inviting way why this place is important to our larger culture. Jane, in addition to having a great laugh and knack for friendship, is vice president of development for a reason—she has drive and makes positive things happen. Nothing languishes under her care. She soon arranged for me to meet a roomful of staff and important volunteers to help me envision what a book like this might contain. Their vision and input got me started and gave me the assurance that, although I loved Mount Auburn and was fairly knowledgeable about the antebellum era that gave it birth, they would be there to help me navigate the considerable complexities of its long history.

Present that morning was volunteer archivist and historian Caroline Loughlin. I sensed she was a quiet supporter of this effort, but I had no idea that she would speak compellingly of the need for this book, and that she would offer to be a generous sponsor of its publication. In time, her generosity would assume greater proportions. Though her recent death cheats us all of the opportunity to properly thank her for her devotion to Mount Auburn, let me point your attention to the dedication page. In his wife's honor, Phillip Loughlin has made a generous grant to support this effort. Getting to know him has been a delight as well.

At that original meeting, we all agreed that either an established press would buy in, or I would not write the book. We brainstormed the possibilities, and as I wrote the book proposal I inwardly hoped that someone at Beacon Press, where I had the pleasure of publishing more than a decade ago, might see in this book the potential we saw in it. That hope was fulfilled when Beacon editor Alexis Rizzuto responded favorably to the proposal. It turned out that she lived near Mount Auburn, walked there most weekends, and knew the place better than I did. There was one big proviso, however—the book Jane and I had first talked about did not appeal to her. She thought, knowing the landscape as she did, that a book of short historical biographies was inadequate to the task.

Alexis asked me to remove myself from my comfort zone and do two things—write in some depth about the birds and trees and flowers and flow of nature, and delve into the deeper ecological meaning of the place today. That was the book she wanted, and she challenged me to create it. When Alexis left daily editing at Beacon, Will Myers smoothly slotted in, and he has strongly encouraged me in both these challenges. I felt immediately comforted in his astute and encouraging style. On a personal level, I am grateful that a smart, liberal press like Beacon exists—but on a societal level, I feel like its success and impact are absolutely essential. It publishes books we need to read, and I have the uneasy feeling that many such books would never reach us without the vision—and guts—of Beacon Press.

Jane introduced me to the two men who have, frankly, revolutionized Mount Auburn: past president William Clendaniel and president David Barnett. They are very different kinds of men, with Clendaniel's historical interests and visionary managerial style playing off of Barnett's horticultural and ecological interests. Together, they have offered what the cemetery needed, enabling it to do more than survive, but to thrive. I can hardly thank David enough for his long talks, walks, and encouragement.

Every member of the staff I interviewed (and rode around in the little electric cars with) was invested and generous with his or her time—notably Dennis Collins, horticultural curator; Paul Walker, superintendent of grounds; and the lively Candace Currie, director of planning and sustainability. Each gave real insight not only into the landscape, but into why they love their jobs. Tom Johnson, family services coordinator, is someone I, as a minister, most relate to, as we both work with people dealing with grievous loss.

Providing more than support—for they did more than submit to questions and help sort through quandaries—were Meg L. Winslow, curator of the historical collections, and Bree Harvey, vice president of cemetery and visitor services (a title that hardly conveys Bree's comprehensive and overarching knowledge of Mount Auburn). Both did grinding editing and fact-checking that I needed. I worked hard on this book, but no amount of research over two years could possibly replace their deep, deep knowledge of the long and complex history here. Without their hard work, this book would read very differently indeed.

In addition, Meg introduced me to her husband, Matt Longo, an architect who happens also to be an outstanding artist. I charged Matt with going out there and responding to the land as I tried to do—to let his artistic instincts be as free as mine. I think you will agree that Matt's wonderful drawings capture something vital about the place, and I am so glad Meg introduced us.

ACKNOWLEDGMENTS

I thank the good people of First Church in Boston, where I happily serve as senior minister. I saw this book as solidly a part of my ministry there, and they gave me freedom to write it.

And I would have written nada—nothing—without the continuing love and support (and wisdom) of my wife, Liz, whom I have the pleasure of going through life with, till death do us part (perhaps maybe longer). Every book I manage to write actually belongs to her. Anyone married to a writer knows what I mean.

NOTES

Abbreviations for frequently cited titles and collections.

AA
Aaron Sachs, *Arcadian America: The Death and Life of an Environmental Tradition* (New Haven, CT: Yale University Press, 2013).

HCMA
Jacob Bigelow, *A History of the Cemetery of Mount Auburn* (orig. 1859; Cambridge, MA: Applewood Books, 1988).

SA
Sweet Auburn: The Magazine of the Friends of Mount Auburn. Available at the website for the Friends of Mount Auburn Cemetery, http://mountauburn.org.

SCH
Blanche M. G. Linden, *Silent City on a Hill: Picturesque Landscapes of Memory and Boston's Mount Auburn Cemetery* (Amherst: University of Massachusetts Press, 2007).

Invocation—Into the Garden

(2) **As resting places**/ in "Death," *Lapham's Quarterly* 6, no. 4 (Fall 2013): 165. (4) **"the tomb is eclipsed"**/ Philippe Aries, *The Hour of Our Death* (New York: Knopf, 1981), 533. (5) **"not only a celebrant"**/ Gary Wills, *Lincoln at Gettysburg* (New York: Simon & Schuster, 1992), 63; see also chapter 2, "Gettysburg and the Culture of Death." (5) **"The contemplation of"**/ Ibid., 73. (6) **"We are still"**/ Thomas Cole, as quoted in *SCH*, 208. (6) **"Eden—the first abode"**/ Quoted in *SCH*, 148. (6) **"let what would pass"**/ Emerson, quoted in *SCH*, 165. (7) **"whose fathers seemed"**/ Harriet Martineau, *Retrospect of Western Travel*, vol. 3 (orig. 1838; New York: Greenwood Press, 1969), 272. (7) **"never with so much"**/ Jane Holtz Kay, *Lost Boston*, rev. ed. (Boston: Houghton Mifflin, 1999) preface, x. (7) **"What is the grave"**/ *HCMA*, 153–54. (8) **"It was as if"**/ Kay, *Lost Boston*, 127. (9) **"a great book of Nature"**/ As quoted in Michael Kammen, *A Time to Every Purpose: The Four Seasons in American Culture* (Chapel Hill: University of North Carolina Press, 2004), 101. (11) **"Second Greatest Idea"**/ Aaron Sachs, "Mt. Auburn's Farsighted Message," *Boston Globe*, January 13, 2013. (12) **"A cemetery ought"**/ Rev. Peter Gomes, address at the 175th anniversary of Mount Auburn's consecration, September 24, 2006.

Consecration Day

(20) **"Mount Auburn has been"**/ *HCMA*, 13. (21) **"Sunk in utter"**/ Louis P. Masur, *1831: Year of Eclipse* (New York: Hill & Wang, 2002), 208. (22) **"A rural cemetery"**/ *HCMA*, 160. (24) **"beautiful composition"**/ Martineau, *Retrospect of Western Travel*, 281. The best biography of Justice Story remains Gerald T. Dunne, *Justice Joseph Story and the Rise of the Supreme Court* (New York: Simon & Schuster, 1970). Story's address in full is an essential cornerstone of understanding Mount Auburn; it can be found in *HCMA*, 143–67. As well, a wonderfully written and illustrated publication of the Friends of Mount Auburn Cemetery gives an evocative introduction to the heart of Mount Auburn: *A Guide to Consecration Dell* (2006), with a definitive essay on its natural history by Christopher Leahy. (30) **"She enthusiastically"**/ *SA* (Fall 2011): 9.

From Crypt to Garden

(32) **"It seemed as if"**/ As quoted in *The Oxford Book of Death*, D. J. Enright, ed. (Oxford, UK: Oxford University Press, 1983), 319. (33) **"St. Mary-

lebone Parish Church"/ Bill Bryson, *At Home: A Short History of Private Life* (New York: Anchor Books, 2011), 319–20. (34) **"I will show you"**/ As quoted in Alfred Kazin, *An American Procession* (New York: Vintage Books, 1985), 3. (34) **"Oh, well, I"**/ *Oxford Book of Death*, 192. (35) **"gross abuses"**/ *HCMA*, 1. The definitive account of the founding of Mount Auburn is chapter 7, "The Cemetery Idea and the Founding of Mount Auburn," in *SCH*, 133–53. (37) **"too little thought"**/ *HCMA*, 137. Everett's entire address is worthy of background reading; see pp. 133–43. A good introduction to a "lost" figure in our history is the section on Everett in Philip B. Kunhardt Jr., *A New Birth of Freedom: Lincoln at Gettysburg* (Boston: Little, Brown, 1983), 185–205. (40) **"more influence on"**/ *SA* (Winter 1986). (42) **improbably, de facto parks**/ Bryson, *At Home*, 321. (42) **"gradually, it dawned"**/ Ibid., 322. (43) **"their book of history"**/ Catharine Arnold, *Necropolis: London and Its Dead* (London: Pocket Books, 2006), 91–92. (44) **"The Garden also"**/ *HCMA*, 173. (44) **As he and surveyor** / *AA*, 20, 39. (45) **"in a few years"**/ *HCMA*, 108–10.

Finding Yourself Lost

(46) **"Mount Auburn is not"**/ *SA* (Fall 1994). (46) **As he hastened**/ Bernard Malamud, *Dubin's Lives* (New York: Penguin, 1979), 12–13. (47) **Horowitz's On Looking**/ See Alexandra Horowitz, *On Looking: A Walker's Guide* (New York: Scribner, 2013). (49) **"till the children"**/ Henry David Thoreau, "Walking," available at multiple online sources. (50) **"so curved and winding"**/ *AA*, 35. (50) **"Cycles are circles"**/ Quoted in Kammen, *A Time to Every Purpose*, frontispiece. (51) **"Nature can only"**/ As quoted in Perry Miller, *Errand into the Wilderness* (Cambridge, MA: Belknap Press of Harvard University Press, 1956), 197. (51) **"almost magically"**/ *AA*, 39. (52) **"Why did the core"**/ Ibid., 15. (53) **"I have been able"**/ *AA*, 25. (54) **"To lose yourself"**/ As quoted in Rebecca Solnit, *A Field Guide to Getting Lost* (New York: Penguin, 2005), 6. (56) **"It is a surprising"**/ Ibid., 14.

A New Manifestation

(57) **"In the years"**/ Megan Marshall, *Margaret Fuller: A New American Life* (New York: Houghton Mifflin Harcourt, 2013), 390. See also John Matteson, *The Lives of Margaret Fuller: A Biography* (New York: Norton, 2012). (57) **"We would have"**/ Unitarian Universalist Association, *Singing the Living Tradition* (Boston: Unitarian Universalist Association, 1993), 575. (58) **"I**

accept"/ Perry Miller, ed., *Margaret Fuller, American Romantic* (Ithaca, NY: Cornell University Press, 1963), ix. (58) **"I know all"**/ Ibid. (58) **"She had only"**/ Quoted in Paula Blanchard, *Margaret Fuller: From Transcendentalism to Revolution* (orig. 1978; Reading, MA: Addison-Wesley, 1987), 339. (60) **"the river so slow"**/ *AA*, 75. (60) **"Spent the afternoon"**/ *AA*, 81. (61) **"we are all a little"**/ David S. Reynolds, *Waking Giant: America in the Age of Jackson* (New York: Harper Perennial, 2008), 157. (62) **"The terror of death"**/ Masur, *1831*, 207. (62) **"Never, perhaps"**/ Ibid., 12. (63) **"If the Jacksonian"**/ Reynolds, *Waking Giant*, 383. (63) **"What may seem"**/ Stephen Kendrick and Paul Kendrick, *Sarah's Long Walk: The Free Blacks of Boston and How Their Struggle for Equality Changed America* (Boston: Beacon Press, 2004), 55. There is a need for a modern biography of William Ellery Channing. Though difficult to find, the two best resources remain Arthur W. Brown, *Always Young for Liberty: A Biography of William Ellery Channing* (Syracuse, NY: Syracuse University Press, 1956), and Jack Mendelsohn, *Channing, the Reluctant Radical: A Biography* (New York: Praeger, 1980). (65) **"I come as the advocate"** / Dorothea L. Dix, *Memorial to the Legislature of Massachusetts, 1843*, Internet Archive, https://archive.org/stream/memorialtolegisloodixd#page/n3 /mode/2up. For the life of Dix, see David Gollaher, *Voice for the Mad: The Life of Dorothea Dix* (New York: Free Press, 1995), and Dorothy Clarke Wilson, *Stranger and Traveler: The Story of Dorothea Dix, American Reformer* (Boston: Little, Brown, 1975). (69) **"It is better to die"**/ As quoted in E. Fuller Torrey, *The Martyrdom of Abolitionist Charles Torrey* (Baton Rouge: Louisiana State University Press, 2013), 199. See also Melissa Banta, *African American Heritage Trail* (Cambridge, MA: Friends of Mount Auburn Cemetery, 2013), 16–17.

An Earthly Paradise

(70) **"coming up out"**/ Quoted in George H. Williams, *Wilderness and Paradise in Christian Thought: The Biblical Experience of the Desert in the History of Christianity and the Paradise Theme in the Theological Idea of the University* (New York: Harper and Brothers, 1962), 100. (70) **"The word Paradise"**/ Ibid., 11. (72) **"Looking forward"**/ Witold Rybczynski, *A Clearing in the Distance: Frederick Law Olmsted and America in the Nineteenth Century* (New York: Simon & Schuster, 1999), 22. See also Justin Martin, *Genius of Place: The Life of Frederick Law Olmsted* (Cambridge, MA: Da Capo Press, 2011). (73) **"The true policy"**/ Robert Twombly, ed. *Andrew Jackson Downing: Essential Texts* (New York: Norton, 2012), 218–22, and see the entirety of Twombly's short es-

say "A Talk About Public Parks and Gardens." (75) **"No sooner was"**/ Twombly, "Public Cemeteries and Public Gardens," 231. (76) **"When I go into"**/ Wade Graham, *American Eden: From Monticello to Central Park to Our Backyards; What Our Gardens Tell Us About Who We Are* (New York: HarperCollins, 2011), frontispiece. (76) **"conviction that our"**/ Ibid., xiv. (77) **"a miniature Utopia"**/ Ibid., xii. (77) **"political theories"**/ Ibid. **"how a properly"**/ Ibid., 89.

Sacred Tourists

(81) **"Have you ever"**/ Quoted in *SCH*, 249. (82) **"tourist attractions"**/ John F. Sears, *Sacred Places: American Tourist Attractions in the Nineteenth Century* (New York: Oxford University Press, 1989), 7. (83) **"The way to"**/ Quoted in John Crowley, "Squeak and Gibber," *Lapham's Quarterly* (September 2013): 191. (83) **"The Founders were"**/ Christine A. Hurd, "Dallying with the Dead," *Harvard Crimson*, October 15, 2011. (84) **"The idea of traveling"**/ Sears, *Sacred Places*, 88. (85) **"Together images"**/ *SA* (Winter 2013): 15. (86) **"Today, the cemetery"**/ Lisa Genova, *Still Alice* (New York: Gallery Books, 2009), 75. (86) **"I passed"**/ From an interview in *SA* (Winter 2013): 9. (87) **When roses cease**/ Emily Dickinson, "When Roses Cease to Bloom, Sir." (88) **Because I could not**/ Emily Dickinson, "Because I Could Not Stop for Death." (88) **"Death is too"**/ Jacques Choron, *Death and Western Thought* (New York: Collier Books, 1963), 32. (89) **"Speak not smoothly"**/ Ibid. (89) **"Whatsoever thy hand"**/ Eccles. 9:10. (89) **"Or ever the silver"**/ Ibid., 12:6. (89) **"And many of them"**/ Dan. 12:2. (91) **"There's gold in"**/ Jessica Mitford, *The American Way of Death* (New York: Simon & Schuster, 1963), 97, 119–24.

Frozen Transcendentalism

(98) **"In Cambridge"**/ As quoted in Meg Winslow and Brian Sullivan, eds., *Selected Quotes About Mount Auburn* (Cambridge, MA: Mount Auburn Cemetery Historical Collections publication, 2012). (98) **"When the leaves"**/ Ibid. (100) **"I become a transparent eyeball"**/ Ralph Waldo Emerson, *Nature* (Boston: James Munroe and Company, 1836), https://archive.org/details/naturemunroeooemerrich. (101) **"Would it not be"**/ Nathaniel Hawthorne, *The Blithedale Romance* (1852), in Hawthorne, *Collected Novels* (New York: Library of America, 1983), 746–47. (102) **"I am making"**/ Plotinus, as quoted in Choron, *Death and Western Thought*, 77.

(103) **"after failing in"**/ Kazin, *An American Procession*, 33. (104) **"without sharing"**/ Ibid., 40. (105) **"Went yesterday"**/ Alfred R. Ferguson, ed., *The Journals and Miscellaneous Notebooks of Ralph Waldo Emerson*, vol. IV (Cambridge, MA: Belknap Press of Harvard University Press, 1964), 272–75.

The Rivals

(112) **"separate creation"**/ Christoph Irmscher, *Louis Agassiz: Creator of American Science* (New York: Houghton Mifflin Harcourt, 2013), 176. (112) **"It is poor"**/ A. Hunter Dupree, *Asa Gray: American Botanist, Friend of Darwin* (orig. 1959; Baltimore: Johns Hopkins University Press, 1988), 269. (112) **"as a kind of demagogue"**/ Gertrude Himmelfarb, *Darwin and the Darwinian Revolution* (New York: Norton, 1959), 266–67. (113) **"Mr. Darwin boldly"**/ Dupree, *Asa Gray*, 286. (113) **"There 'the controversy'"**/ Ibid., 323. (114) **"Just fate"**/ As quoted in ibid., 410. (115) **"It seems almost impossible"**/ "Images of Emancipation," *New York Times*, December 20, 2012.

The Poet and the Abolitionist

(116) **"Point of hill"**/ Article on and interview about Robert Creeley's "Stairway to Heaven," *SA* (Winter 2013): 7. (116) **"His sense of connection"**/ Ibid. (117) **"Yesterday I was"**/ Winslow and Sullivan, *Selected Quotes About Mount Auburn*. (117) **"Who, except wretched"**/ Charles C. Calhoun, *Longfellow: A Rediscovered Life* (Boston: Beacon Press, 2004), 255–56. (118) **"Sail on, O Ship"**/ Harry Hansen, *Longfellow's New England* (New York: Hastings House, 1972), 9. (118) **"It is a wonderful"**/ Calhoun, *Longfellow*, 195. (121) **"There is a mountain"**/ Henry Wadsworth Longfellow, "The Cross of Snow." (123) **"I cannot recall"**/ Calhoun, *Longfellow*, 249. (123) **"Did he die"**/ Christoph Irmscher, *Longfellow Redux* (Urbana: University of Illinois Press, 2006), 7. (125) **"Oh! I long"**/ Calhoun, *Longfellow*, 155. (126) **"River, that stealest"**/ As quoted in Christoph Irmscher, *Public Poet, Private Man: Henry Wadsworth Longfellow at 200* (Amherst: University of Massachusetts Press, 2009), 83.

"So Young and Victorious"

(129) **"She and I have"**/ Carol Bundy, *The Nature of Sacrifice: A Biography of Charles Russell Lowell, Jr., 1835–64* (New York: Farrar, Straus and Giroux, 2005), 266. See also Edward Waldo Emerson, ed., *Life and Letters of Charles Russell Lowell* (Boston: Houghton, Mifflin, 1907). (129) **"I would give"**/

Bundy, *Nature of Sacrifice*, 278. (129) **"I looked back"**/ Joan Waugh, *Unsentimental Reformer: The Life of Josephine Shaw Lowell* (Cambridge, MA: Harvard University Press, 1998), 72. (130) **"Rob was very"**/ Bundy, *Nature of Sacrifice*, 314. (130) **"I don't want"**/ Ibid., 456. (132) **"After the war"**/ Waugh, *Unsentimental Reformer*, 85. (132) **honed her skills as**/ Ibid., 8. (132) **"carelessness"** and **"If it could only"**/ William Rhinelander Stewart, *The Philanthropic Work of Josephine Shaw Lowell* (New York: Macmillan, 1911), 130. (133) **"the strong and beautiful"**/ Website of the New York City Department of Parks and Recreation: Josephine Shaw Lowell Memorial Fountain, Bryant Park. (133) **"lonely kind of courage"**/ William James, "Oration at the Exercises in the Boston Music Hall, May 31, 1897, upon the Unveiling of the Shaw Monument," reprinted in "Robert Gould Shaw," in William James, *Memories and Studies* (New York: Longmans, Green, 1911), 57. (134) **"Bowditch supplemented"**/ Drew Gilpin Faust, *This Republic of Suffering: Death and the American Civil War* (New York: Knopf, 2008), 169–70.

Going Over the Ground

(141) **"We must go over"**/ As quoted in Paul Fussell, *The Great War and Modern Memory* (New York: Oxford University Press, 1975), 355.

Mine Eyes Have Seen the Glory

(143) **"so, with a sudden"**/ Julia Ward Howe, *Reminiscences, 1818–1899* (Boston: Houghton Mifflin, 1899), 275–78. (146) **"I have been"**/ Valarie H. Ziegler, *Diva Julia: The Public Romance and Private Agony of Julia Ward Howe* (Harrisburg, PA: Trinity Press, 2003), 105. See also Deborah Pickman Clifford, *Mine Eyes Have Seen the Glory: A Biography of Julia Ward Howe* (Boston: Little, Brown, 1979). (149) **"In the afternoon"**/ Laura E. Richards and Maud Howe Elliott, *Julia Ward Howe: 1819–1910*, vol. II (Boston: Houghton Mifflin, 1916), 290. For a recent biography on Samuel Gridley Howe, see James W. Trent Jr., *The Manliest Man: Samuel G. Howe and the Contours of Nineteenth-Century American Reform* (Amherst: University of Massachusetts Press, 2012).

The Time of the Singing of Birds

(151) **"It is a mazy"**/ Martineau, *Retrospect of Western Travel*, 278–79. (153) **"hallowed shrine"**/ Christopher Leahy and Clare Walker Leslie, *Birds and Birding at Mount Auburn Cemetery* (Cambridge, MA: Friends of Mount

Auburn Cemetery, 2004), 1. (153) **"indeed, the entire region"**/ Ibid., 8. (154) **"the patron saint"**/ Ibid., 10. (155) **"The Dell is"**/ Quoted in an interview for a special issue on birding, *SA* (Spring/Summer 2012), 4. (156) **"I am birdwatching"**/ Simon Barnes, *How to Be a (Bad) Birdwatcher* (London: Short Books, 2004), 17. (157) **"For, lo, the winter"**/ Song of Sol. 2:11.

"My Story Ends in Freedom . . ."

(158) **"he fled to Boston"**/ Banta, *African American Heritage Trail*, 18. (160) **"Her heart is"**/ Sydney Nathans, *To Free a Family: The Journey of Mary Walker* (Cambridge, MA: Harvard University Press, 2012), 159. (161) **"wild with joy"**/ Ibid., 217. (161) **"Slavery is terrible"**/ Quoted in Harriet A. Jacobs, *Incidents in the Life of a Slave Girl: Written by Herself*, ed. Jean Yellin (orig. 1861; Cambridge, MA: Harvard University Press, 2000), xxviii. See also Jean Yellin, *Harriet Jacobs: A Life* (New York: Basic Civitas, 2004). (163) **"Patient in tribulation"**/ Banta, *African American Heritage Trail*, 11. (165) **"deepest and most"**/ Kendrick and Kendrick, *Sarah's Long Walk*, 257. (165) **"Reader, my story"**/ Jacobs, *Incidents in the Life of a Slave Girl*, 201.

Grave Words

(167) **"Blessed Lord, what"**/ From the monument of David McCord, Mount Auburn Cemetery.

Greening

(176) **"Decay! Decay!"**/ *HCMA*, 204. (178) **"The progress of"**/ Ibid., 176, 191. (179) **"Could we, by"**/ Ibid., 193. (180) **"I think we're finally"**/ From a transcript of Mark Harris's presentation at Mount Auburn, June 14, 2014. (181) **"The finishing touches"**/ *SA* (Winter 2002): 1–3. (185) **"It is a wonderful"**/ Interview with Julie Moir Messervy, *SA* (Fall 2011): 2. (186) **"This landscape"**/ David Shore, as quoted in *Changing Tastes* audio walking tour, available at Mount Auburn visitor services and at http://mountauburn .toursphere.com/en/changing-tastes-8765.html.

Melting Art

(187) **"The stones in this"**/ Richard E. Meyer, *Cemeteries and Gravemarkers: Voices of American Culture* (Logan: Utah State University Press, 1992), 1. (187) **"Here may be found"**/ Ibid., 5. (188) **"I am not satisfied"**/ Arnold,

Necropolis, 219. (189) **"with broken columns"**/ Ibid., 216. (190) **"that vile and pagan"**/ As quoted in ibid., 222. (191) **"tell the truth"**/ Carl Watkins, *The Undiscovered Country: Journeys Among the Dead* (London: Bodley Head, 2013), 147. (193) **"It is without question"**/ The website of the Friends of Mount Auburn Cemetery (http://mountauburn.org), articles on the restoration of the Binney monument. (194) **"Some praise me"**/ Banta, *African American Heritage Trail*, 44.

Call Me Trimtab

(197) **the first engineer saint**/ Thomas T. K. Zung, *Buckminster Fuller: Anthology for the New Millennium* (New York: St. Martin's Griffin, 2002), 362. (198) **"He is placed"**/ As quoted in Hugh Kenner, *Bucky: A Guided Tour of Buckminster Fuller* (New York: William Morrow, 1973), 147. (198) **"a comprehensive"**/ Ibid., 81. (199) **"an encouraging example"**/ Zung, *Buckminster Fuller*, 283. See also Lloyd Steven Sieden, *Buckminster Fuller's Universe: An Appreciation* (Cambridge, MA: Perseus Books, 2000).

The Experimental Garden

(202) **"Boston was left"**/ Van Wyck Brooks, *New England: Indian Summer* (Cleveland: World Publishing, 1946), 423. (202) **"The Boston of"**/ Edward Everett Hale, *James Russell Lowell and His Friends* (orig. 1899; New York: Chelsea House, 1980), 265. (203) **"I own a villa"**/ Quoted in the 175th Anniversary Friends of Mount Auburn booklet, 23. (204) **"I cannot conceive"**/ John Marquand, *The Late George Apley* (orig. 1937; New York: Little, Brown, 2004), 237–39. (205) **"The Legislature"**/ HCMA, 163. (206) **"build landscapes"**/ Graham, *American Eden*, 303. (206) **Isamu Noguchi**/ Ibid., 323. (207) **"new pastoral urbanism"**/ Ibid., 403. (213) **"the complex internal"**/ John Fowles, *The Tree* (Boston: Little, Brown, 1979), 34–36, 74–76. (216) **"it is in vain"**/ Kammen, *A Time to Every Purpose*, 36.

The Sphinx

(220) **"fifteen feet long"**/ Jacob Bigelow, *An Account of the Sphinx at Mount Auburn* (Boston: Little, Brown, 1872), 13. (221) **"What symbol can"**/ Bigelow, *An Account of the Sphinx*, 13–14. (221) **"express, though imperfectly"**/ Ibid., 5–6. See also Banta, *African American Heritage Trail*, 48–49. (221) **the freeing of 3.5 million**/ Civil War Home Page, http://www.civil-war.net/.

NOTES

(224) **"The world rolls round"**/ Emerson, "May-Day," from *May-Day and Other Pieces* (Boston: Ticknor and Fields, 1867).

Epilogue—A New Adam and Eve

(226) **"for instance, let us"**/ Nathaniel Hawthorne, "A New Adam and Eve," in Hawthorne, *Tales and Sketches* (orig. 1843; New York: Library of America, 1982), 746, 761–63. (228) **"For a transitory enchanted"**/ Kazin, *An American Procession*, 397.